TEACHER'S PET PUBLICATIONS

PUZZLE PACK
for
Stargirl

based on the book by
Jerry Spinielli

Written by
Mary B. Collins

INTRODUCTION
If you already own the LitPlan for this title, this Puzzle Pack will refresh your Unit Resource Materials and Vocabulary Resource Materials sections plus give you additional materials you can substitute into the tests.If you do not already have a complete LitPlan, these pages will give you some supplemental materials to use with your own plan. There are two main groups of materials: one set for unit words (such as characters' names, symbols, places, etc.) and one set for vocabulary words associated with the book.

WORD LIST
There is a word list for both the unit words and the vocabulary words. These lists show you which words are being used in the materials and the clues or definitions being used for those words. You may want to give students a word list with clues/definitions to help them, or you may want students to only have a word list (without clues/definitions) if you want them to work a little harder. Both are available for duplication. The word lists can also be your "calling key" for the bingo games.

FILL IN THE BLANK AND MATCHING
There are 4 each of the fill in the blank and matching worksheets for both the unit and vocabulary words. These pages can be used either as extra worksheets for students or as objective parts of a unit test. They can be done individually if students need extra help or as a whole class activity to review the material covered.

MAGIC SQUARES
The magic squares not only reinforce the material covered but also work on reasoning and math skills. Many teachers have told us that their students really enjoy doing these!

WORD SEARCH PUZZLES
The word search words go in all directions, as indicated on your answer keys. Two of the word search puzzles have the clues listed rather than the words. This makes the puzzle a little more difficult, but it reinforces the material better. Two word search puzzles have words only for students who find the clue puzzles too difficult.

CROSSWORD PUZZLES
Both unit and vocabulary word sections have 4 crossword puzzles.

BINGO CARDS
There are 32 individual bingo cards for the unit words and 32 individual bingo cards for the vocabulary words. You can use your word list as a "call list," calling the words at random and marking them off of your list as you go, or you could use the flash cards by cutting them apart and drawing the words at random from a hat (or box or whatever). To make a better review, you might ask for the definition and spelling of each word as you call it out–or you could call out the definitions and have students tell you the words they need to look for on the puzzle.

JUGGLE LETTERS
The vocabulary juggle letter game is intended to help students learn the spellings of the words. One sheet has the definitions listed on it as an extra help for students who need it or to reinforce the definitions if you choose to do so.

FLASH CARDS
We've included a set of vocabulary flash cards you can duplicate, cut, and fold for your students. Some teachers make a few sets for general use by the class; others make a set for each student. Some teachers duplicate them for each student and have the students cut & fold their own. You can cut out just the words and put them in a hat, have each student pick out one word and write the definition and a sentence for that word. Students then swap words and papers, with the next student adding a sentence of his own under the last one. You can have students swap as many times as you like. Each time the student will read the sentences written prior to his own and then add a sentence. You can cut out the words and definitions separately and play "I Have; Who Has?" Each student in the room draws a word and definition. The first student says, "I have (the name of the word). Who has the definition?" The student with the definition reads it then says, "I have (the name of the vocabulary word she has). Who has the definition?" The round continues until all words and definitions have been given.

Stargirl Unit Word List

No.	Word	Clue/Definition
1.	ARCHIE	Professor and friend to students
2.	BARNEY	60 million year old Paleocene rodent
3.	BASKETBALL	This MAHS team had a winning streak
4.	BIKE	Danny's new one went into the trash
5.	BONE	Loyal Order of the Stone ____
6.	BORLOCK	Leo's last name
7.	BUNNY	Dance Stargirl led; ___ Hop
8.	CACTUS	Senor Saguaro
9.	CARAWAY	Stargirl's last name
10.	CARD	Leo's Valentine ____ said: I love you
11.	CHANGE	Leo wanted Stargirl to do this
12.	CHEERLEADER	Stargirl was invited to become one
13.	CHICKENS	Don't count yours until they're hatched
14.	CHICO	Hand held camera and its operator for Hot Seat
15.	CHOOSE	Leo had to ___ between Stargirl and his friends
16.	DANNY	He broke his leg in a bike accident
17.	DORI	Stargirl's 9th grade friend
18.	DRIVER	Stargirl spent the 4th quarter of the Red Rock game outside talking to the bus ____
19.	ELECTRONS	Name of MAHS sports teams
20.	ENCHANTED	Stargirl showed Leo an ____ place in the desert
21.	EVELYN	Fictitious ordinary person: ___ Everybody
22.	FILLER	Part of the newspaper Stargirl read
23.	FLOAT	Stargirl's bike and sidecar looked like a parade ___
24.	FROGS	The students were like mud ___ awakening
25.	FUNERAL	Stargirl went to Anna's grandfather's
26.	GLENDALE	Team MAHS lost to in the playoffs
27.	GOALPOST	Stargirl climbed it at the football game
28.	GREETING	Stargirl made her own ___ cards
29.	HEART	Her eyes went straight to her ___
30.	HERO	After the state oratorical contest, Susan expected to be welcomed back like one
31.	HILLARI	Miss Kimble; she dangled the rat
32.	JURY	Hot Seat panel asking questions
33.	KEVIN	Hot Seat anchor
34.	KOVAC	Sun Valley's injured star player
35.	LIGHT	When Stargirl cries, she does not shed tears, but this
36.	LUNCH	Time when Stargirl sang Happy Birthday
37.	MARICOPAS	The mountains
38.	MCSHANE	Teacher who drove Susan and Leo to the state contest
39.	MICA	____ Area High School
40.	MOA	Large, extinct bird
41.	MOB	The Hot Seat jurors turned into a ___
42.	MOCKINGBIRD	Bird that imitates the sounds of other birds
43.	MOVED	What Stargirl's family did after the ball
44.	MUDPIE	Another Susan alias
45.	NECKTIE	Porcupine ____
46.	OCOTILLO	Ball where Stargirl regained her popularity
47.	ORATORICAL	Kind of contest Stargirl entered
48.	ORDINARY	For a person so different, Stargirl's house was ___
49.	PARR	Wayne's last name

No.	Word	Clue/Definition
50.	PETER	Stargirl made a scrapbook for him
51.	PLATE	Silver contest award
52.	PLEDGE	Stargirl said an unusual ___ of Allegiance
53.	RAT	Cinnamon was one
54.	RAYMOND	First to dance with Stargirl
55.	REGAL	Word some parents used to describe Stargirl's appearance at the ball
56.	ROBINEAU	Faculty adviser for Hot Seat
57.	ROCK	MAHS basketball team massacred the Red ___ team
58.	SEAT	Hot ___
59.	SENSES	Sometimes we need to erase them
60.	SHUNNED	The students did this to Stargirl and Leo
61.	SONORAN	The ___ desert
62.	SPINELLI	Author
63.	STALKING	Leah thought Stargirl's card game was like ___
64.	STARBOY	Leo
65.	STARGIRL	Susan's alias
66.	SUNFLOWER	Club requiring members to do nice things for others
67.	TOMATO	Someone threw one in Stargirl's face
68.	TOOLSHED	Archie's ___ was Stargirl's office
69.	UKEE	___ Dooks
70.	UKULELE	Stargirl's instrument
71.	WAGON	The Happy___held pebbles
72.	WAYNE	Hillari's boyfriend
73.	WIN	MAHS basketball team fans expected to ___

1. Sun Valley's injured star player

2. Leo had to ___ between Stargirl and his friends

3. Stargirl's instrument

4. Her eyes went straight to her ___

5. Stargirl showed Leo an ____ place in the desert

6. When Stargirl cries, she does not shed tears, but this

7. Leah thought Stargirl's card game was like ___

8. Danny's new one went into the trash

9. Hot ___

10. ____ Area High School

11. Dance Stargirl led; ___ Hop

12. Leo

13. Teacher who drove Susan and Leo to the state contest

14. For a person so different, Stargirl's house was ___

15. Don't count yours until they're hatched

16. Ball where Stargirl regained her popularity

17. First to dance with Stargirl

18. Fictitious ordinary person: ___ Everybody

19. Time when Stargirl sang Happy Birthday

20. Stargirl's bike and sidecar looked like a parade ___

KOVAC	1. Sun Valley's injured star player
CHOOSE	2. Leo had to ___ between Stargirl and his friends
UKULELE	3. Stargirl's instrument
HEART	4. Her eyes went straight to her ___
ENCHANTED	5. Stargirl showed Leo an ____ place in the desert
LIGHT	6. When Stargirl cries, she does not shed tears, but this
STALKING	7. Leah thought Stargirl's card game was like ___
BIKE	8. Danny's new one went into the trash
SEAT	9. Hot ___
MICA	10. ____ Area High School
BUNNY	11. Dance Stargirl led; ___ Hop
STARBOY	12. Leo
MCSHANE	13. Teacher who drove Susan and Leo to the state contest
ORDINARY	14. For a person so different, Stargirl's house was ___
CHICKENS	15. Don't count yours until they're hatched
OCOTILLO	16. Ball where Stargirl regained her popularity
RAYMOND	17. First to dance with Stargirl
EVELYN	18. Fictitious ordinary person: ___ Everybody
LUNCH	19. Time when Stargirl sang Happy Birthday
FLOAT	20. Stargirl's bike and sidecar looked like a parade ___

1. The students were like mud ___ awakening

2. Word some parents used to describe Stargirl's appearance at the ball

3. ___ Dooks

4. Silver contest award

5. Bird that imitates the sounds of other birds

6. The Happy___held pebbles

7. The ___ desert

8. Kind of contest Stargirl entered

9. Teacher who drove Susan and Leo to the state contest

10. For a person so different, Stargirl's house was ___

11. Cinnamon was one

12. Time when Stargirl sang Happy Birthday

13. After the state oratorical contest, Susan expected to be welcomed back like one

14. Danny's new one went into the trash

15. Leah thought Stargirl's card game was like ___

16. Hillari's boyfriend

17. The Hot Seat jurors turned into a ___

18. Stargirl spent the 4th quarter of the Red Rock game outside talking to the bus ____

19. Stargirl made her own ___ cards

20. Ball where Stargirl regained her popularity

FROGS	1. The students were like mud ___ awakening
REGAL	2. Word some parents used to describe Stargirl's appearance at the ball
UKEE	3. ___ Dooks
PLATE	4. Silver contest award
MOCKINGBIRD	5. Bird that imitates the sounds of other birds
WAGON	6. The Happy___ held pebbles
SONORAN	7. The ___ desert
ORATORICAL	8. Kind of contest Stargirl entered
MCSHANE	9. Teacher who drove Susan and Leo to the state contest
ORDINARY	10. For a person so different, Stargirl's house was ___
RAT	11. Cinnamon was one
LUNCH	12. Time when Stargirl sang Happy Birthday
HERO	13. After the state oratorical contest, Susan expected to be welcomed back like one
BIKE	14. Danny's new one went into the trash
STALKING	15. Leah thought Stargirl's card game was like ___
WAYNE	16. Hillari's boyfriend
MOB	17. The Hot Seat jurors turned into a ___
DRIVER	18. Stargirl spent the 4th quarter of the Red Rock game outside talking to the bus ___
GREETING	19. Stargirl made her own ___ cards
OCOTILLO	20. Ball where Stargirl regained her popularity

1. Stargirl showed Leo an _____ place in the desert

2. For a person so different, Stargirl's house was ___

3. Danny's new one went into the trash

4. The students were like mud ___ awakening

5. Club requiring members to do nice things for others

6. Stargirl made a scrapbook for him

7. Archie's ___ was Stargirl's office

8. Stargirl spent the 4th quarter of the Red Rock game outside talking to the bus _____

9. Porcupine _____

10. Part of the newspaper Stargirl read

11. Dance Stargirl led; ___ Hop

12. After the state oratorical contest, Susan expected to be welcomed back like one

13. Stargirl's 9th grade friend

14. What Stargirl's family did after the ball

15. Time when Stargirl sang Happy Birthday

16. Susan's alias

17. Stargirl was invited to become one

18. Hand held camera and its operator for Hot Seat

19. Leo's Valentine _____said: I love you

20. Stargirl's instrument

ENCHANTED

ORDINARY

BIKE

FROGS

SUNFLOWER

PETER

TOOLSHED

DRIVER

NECKTIE

FILLER

BUNNY

HERO

DORI

MOVED

LUNCH

STARGIRL

CHEERLEADER

CHICO

CARD

UKULELE

1. Stargirl showed Leo an _____ place in the desert

2. For a person so different, Stargirl's house was ___

3. Danny's new one went into the trash

4. The students were like mud ___ awakening

5. Club requiring members to do nice things for others

6. Stargirl made a scrapbook for him

7. Archie's ___ was Stargirl's office

8. Stargirl spent the 4th quarter of the Red Rock game outside talking to the bus ____

9. Porcupine _____

10. Part of the newspaper Stargirl read

11. Dance Stargirl led; ___ Hop

12. After the state oratorical contest, Susan expected to be welcomed back like one

13. Stargirl's 9th grade friend

14. What Stargirl's family did after the ball

15. Time when Stargirl sang Happy Birthday

16. Susan's alias

17. Stargirl was invited to become one

18. Hand held camera and its operator for Hot Seat

19. Leo's Valentine ____said: I love you

20. Stargirl's instrument

____

____

____

____

____

____

____

____

____

____

____

____

____

____

____

____

____

____

____

____

1. Teacher who drove Susan and Leo to the state contest

2. First to dance with Stargirl

3. Dance Stargirl led; ___ Hop

4. Susan's alias

5. Ball where Stargirl regained her popularity

6. The Hot Seat jurors turned into a ___

7. Hand held camera and its operator for Hot Seat

8. Fictitious ordinary person: ___ Everybody

9. After the state oratorical contest, Susan expected to be welcomed back like one

10. MAHS basketball team massacred the Red ___ team

11. The students did this to Stargirl and Leo

12. Stargirl climbed it at the football game

13. Team MAHS lost to in the playoffs

14. Hot Seat anchor

15. Club requiring members to do nice things for others

16. Name of MAHS sports teams

17. Part of the newspaper Stargirl read

18. Archie's ___ was Stargirl's office

19. When Stargirl cries, she does not shed tears, but this

20. Leo's last name

MCSHANE	1. Teacher who drove Susan and Leo to the state contest
RAYMOND	2. First to dance with Stargirl
BUNNY	3. Dance Stargirl led; ___ Hop
STARGIRL	4. Susan's alias
OCOTILLO	5. Ball where Stargirl regained her popularity
MOB	6. The Hot Seat jurors turned into a ___
CHICO	7. Hand held camera and its operator for Hot Seat
EVELYN	8. Fictitious ordinary person: ___ Everybody
HERO	9. After the state oratorical contest, Susan expected to be welcomed back like one
ROCK	10. MAHS basketball team massacred the Red ___ team
SHUNNED	11. The students did this to Stargirl and Leo
GOALPOST	12. Stargirl climbed it at the football game
GLENDALE	13. Team MAHS lost to in the playoffs
KEVIN	14. Hot Seat anchor
SUNFLOWER	15. Club requiring members to do nice things for others
ELECTRONS	16. Name of MAHS sports teams
FILLER	17. Part of the newspaper Stargirl read
TOOLSHED	18. Archie's ___ was Stargirl's office
LIGHT	19. When Stargirl cries, she does not shed tears, but this
BORLOCK	20. Leo's last name

Stargirl Matching 1

___ 1. ENCHANTED   A. Stargirl's instrument

___ 2. FILLER   B. ___ Dooks

___ 3. PLEDGE   C. Stargirl spent the 4th quarter of the Red Rock game
                             outside talking to the bus ____

___ 4. MICA   D. Author

___ 5. WIN   E. After the state oratorical contest, Susan expected to be
                             welcomed back like one

___ 6. WAGON   F. Stargirl showed Leo an ____ place in the desert

___ 7. DRIVER   G. Part of the newspaper Stargirl read

___ 8. FROGS   H. Porcupine _____

___ 9. PARR   I. Miss Kimble; she dangled the rat

___10. LIGHT   J. ____ Area High School

___11. SONORAN   K. The ___ desert

___12. HILLARI   L. Cinnamon was one

___13. NECKTIE   M. MAHS basketball team fans expected to ___

___14. FLOAT   N. When Stargirl cries, she does not shed tears, but this

___15. MOA   O. Hot ___

___16. RAYMOND   P. Stargirl's bike and sidecar looked like a parade ___

___17. HERO   Q. Wayne's last name

___18. UKULELE   R. The students were like mud ___ awakening

___19. RAT   S. First to dance with Stargirl

___20. SEAT   T. Large, extinct bird

___21. ORDINARY   U. Name of MAHS sports teams

___22. SPINELLI   V. For a person so different, Stargirl's house was ___

___23. UKEE   W. Stargirl said an unusual ___ of Allegiance

___24. ELECTRONS   X. The Happy___held pebbles

___25. BIKE   Y. Danny's new one went into the trash

Stargirl Matching 1 Answer Key

F - 1. ENCHANTED	A. Stargirl's instrument
G - 2. FILLER	B. ___ Dooks
W - 3. PLEDGE	C. Stargirl spent the 4th quarter of the Red Rock game outside talking to the bus ____
J - 4. MICA	D. Author
M - 5. WIN	E. After the state oratorical contest, Susan expected to be welcomed back like one
X - 6. WAGON	F. Stargirl showed Leo an ____ place in the desert
C - 7. DRIVER	G. Part of the newspaper Stargirl read
R - 8. FROGS	H. Porcupine _____
Q - 9. PARR	I. Miss Kimble; she dangled the rat
N -10. LIGHT	J. ____ Area High School
K -11. SONORAN	K. The ___ desert
I - 12. HILLARI	L. Cinnamon was one
H -13. NECKTIE	M. MAHS basketball team fans expected to ___
P -14. FLOAT	N. When Stargirl cries, she does not shed tears, but this
T -15. MOA	O. Hot ____
S -16. RAYMOND	P. Stargirl's bike and sidecar looked like a parade ___
E -17. HERO	Q. Wayne's last name
A -18. UKULELE	R. The students were like mud ___ awakening
L - 19. RAT	S. First to dance with Stargirl
O -20. SEAT	T. Large, extinct bird
V -21. ORDINARY	U. Name of MAHS sports teams
D -22. SPINELLI	V. For a person so different, Stargirl's house was ___
B -23. UKEE	W. Stargirl said an unusual ___ of Allegiance
U -24. ELECTRONS	X. The Happy___held pebbles
Y -25. BIKE	Y. Danny's new one went into the trash

Stargirl Matching 2

___ 1. GLENDALE

___ 2. FILLER

___ 3. MARICOPAS

___ 4. ELECTRONS

___ 5. TOOLSHED

___ 6. CARAWAY

___ 7. SPINELLI

___ 8. WAGON

___ 9. CARD

___10. PLATE

___11. BARNEY

___12. CHICO

___13. WAYNE

___14. KOVAC

___15. CHICKENS

___16. PLEDGE

___17. SHUNNED

___18. UKULELE

___19. CHANGE

___20. WIN

___21. DRIVER

___22. HERO

___23. FLOAT

___24. ROBINEAU

___25. NECKTIE

A. Sun Valley's injured star player

B. Hillari's boyfriend

C. Don't count yours until they're hatched

D. Leo's Valentine ____said: I love you

E. The Happy___held pebbles

F. Name of MAHS sports teams

G. The students did this to Stargirl and Leo

H. Hand held camera and its operator for Hot Seat

I. Stargirl said an unusual ___ of Allegiance

J. Stargirl's bike and sidecar looked like a parade ___

K. Part of the newspaper Stargirl read

L. Author

M. Archie's ___ was Stargirl's office

N. Stargirl spent the 4th quarter of the Red Rock game outside talking to the bus ____

O. Stargirl's last name

P. MAHS basketball team fans expected to ___

Q. After the state oratorical contest, Susan expected to be welcomed back like one

R. Team MAHS lost to in the playoffs

S. Leo wanted Stargirl to do this

T. Porcupine _____

U. The mountains

V. 60 million year old Paleocene rodent

W. Silver contest award

X. Faculty adviser for Hot Seat

Y. Stargirl's instrument

Stargirl Matching 2 Answer Key

R - 1. GLENDALE

K - 2. FILLER

U - 3. MARICOPAS

F - 4. ELECTRONS

M - 5. TOOLSHED

O - 6. CARAWAY

L - 7. SPINELLI

E - 8. WAGON

D - 9. CARD

W -10. PLATE

V -11. BARNEY

H -12. CHICO

B -13. WAYNE

A -14. KOVAC

C -15. CHICKENS

I - 16. PLEDGE

G -17. SHUNNED

Y - 18. UKULELE

S - 19. CHANGE

P -20. WIN

N -21. DRIVER

Q -22. HERO

J - 23. FLOAT

X -24. ROBINEAU

T -25. NECKTIE

A. Sun Valley's injured star player

B. Hillari's boyfriend

C. Don't count yours until they're hatched

D. Leo's Valentine ____ said: I love you

E. The Happy___ held pebbles

F. Name of MAHS sports teams

G. The students did this to Stargirl and Leo

H. Hand held camera and its operator for Hot Seat

I. Stargirl said an unusual ___ of Allegiance

J. Stargirl's bike and sidecar looked like a parade ___

K. Part of the newspaper Stargirl read

L. Author

M. Archie's ___ was Stargirl's office

N. Stargirl spent the 4th quarter of the Red Rock game outside talking to the bus ____

O. Stargirl's last name

P. MAHS basketball team fans expected to ___

Q. After the state oratorical contest, Susan expected to be welcomed back like one

R. Team MAHS lost to in the playoffs

S. Leo wanted Stargirl to do this

T. Porcupine ______

U. The mountains

V. 60 million year old Paleocene rodent

W. Silver contest award

X. Faculty adviser for Hot Seat

Y. Stargirl's instrument

Stargirl Matching 3

___ 1. HEART

___ 2. WAGON

___ 3. BIKE

___ 4. CHEERLEADER

___ 5. NECKTIE

___ 6. CHICO

___ 7. HILLARI

___ 8. PARR

___ 9. BASKETBALL

___10. ENCHANTED

___11. STALKING

___12. WAYNE

___13. LUNCH

___14. MOB

___15. SUNFLOWER

___16. PLEDGE

___17. BORLOCK

___18. ARCHIE

___19. ROBINEAU

___20. SEAT

___21. MARICOPAS

___22. STARBOY

___23. MUDPIE

___24. PETER

___25. MOCKINGBIRD

A. Faculty adviser for Hot Seat

B. Stargirl showed Leo an _____ place in the desert

C. Club requiring members to do nice things for others

D. The Happy___ held pebbles

E. Bird that imitates the sounds of other birds

F. Stargirl was invited to become one

G. Danny's new one went into the trash

H. The Hot Seat jurors turned into a ___

I. Hillari's boyfriend

J. Stargirl said an unusual ___ of Allegiance

K. Leah thought Stargirl's card game was like ___

L. Porcupine _____

M. Hand held camera and its operator for Hot Seat

N. This MAHS team had a winning streak

O. Miss Kimble; she dangled the rat

P. Hot ___

Q. The mountains

R. Leo's last name

S. Her eyes went straight to her ___

T. Time when Stargirl sang Happy Birthday

U. Wayne's last name

V. Professor and friend to students

W. Another Susan alias

X. Stargirl made a scrapbook for him

Y. Leo

S - 1. HEART		A. Faculty adviser for Hot Seat
D - 2. WAGON		B. Stargirl showed Leo an ____ place in the desert
G - 3. BIKE		C. Club requiring members to do nice things for others
F - 4. CHEERLEADER		D. The Happy___held pebbles
L - 5. NECKTIE		E. Bird that imitates the sounds of other birds
M - 6. CHICO		F. Stargirl was invited to become one
O - 7. HILLARI		G. Danny's new one went into the trash
U - 8. PARR		H. The Hot Seat jurors turned into a ___
N - 9. BASKETBALL		I. Hillari's boyfriend
B -10. ENCHANTED		J. Stargirl said an unusual ___ of Allegiance
K -11. STALKING		K. Leah thought Stargirl's card game was like ___
I - 12. WAYNE		L. Porcupine _____
T -13. LUNCH		M. Hand held camera and its operator for Hot Seat
H -14. MOB		N. This MAHS team had a winning streak
C -15. SUNFLOWER		O. Miss Kimble; she dangled the rat
J - 16. PLEDGE		P. Hot ___
R -17. BORLOCK		Q. The mountains
V -18. ARCHIE		R. Leo's last name
A -19. ROBINEAU		S. Her eyes went straight to her ___
P -20. SEAT		T. Time when Stargirl sang Happy Birthday
Q -21. MARICOPAS		U. Wayne's last name
Y -22. STARBOY		V. Professor and friend to students
W -23. MUDPIE		W. Another Susan alias
X -24. PETER		X. Stargirl made a scrapbook for him
E -25. MOCKINGBIRD		Y. Leo

Stargirl Matching 4

___ 1. ROBINEAU

___ 2. ARCHIE

___ 3. STALKING

___ 4. RAT

___ 5. BIKE

___ 6. ROCK

___ 7. LIGHT

___ 8. BASKETBALL

___ 9. CACTUS

___10. FILLER

___11. STARGIRL

___12. MARICOPAS

___13. FLOAT

___14. SPINELLI

___15. SEAT

___16. PARR

___17. PLATE

___18. DORI

___19. BORLOCK

___20. ENCHANTED

___21. NECKTIE

___22. ORDINARY

___23. GLENDALE

___24. WAGON

___25. BUNNY

A. Leah thought Stargirl's card game was like ___

B. Danny's new one went into the trash

C. Susan's alias

D. Stargirl showed Leo an ____ place in the desert

E. When Stargirl cries, she does not shed tears, but this

F. Professor and friend to students

G. Cinnamon was one

H. For a person so different, Stargirl's house was ___

I. MAHS basketball team massacred the Red ___ team

J. Hot ___

K. Team MAHS lost to in the playoffs

L. Silver contest award

M. The mountains

N. Part of the newspaper Stargirl read

O. Wayne's last name

P. Faculty adviser for Hot Seat

Q. Porcupine _____

R. The Happy___held pebbles

S. Author

T. Stargirl's bike and sidecar looked like a parade ___

U. Leo's last name

V. Stargirl's 9th grade friend

W. Senor Saguaro

X. This MAHS team had a winning streak

Y. Dance Stargirl led; ___ Hop

P - 1. ROBINEAU	A. Leah thought Stargirl's card game was like ____
F - 2. ARCHIE	B. Danny's new one went into the trash
A - 3. STALKING	C. Susan's alias
G - 4. RAT	D. Stargirl showed Leo an ____ place in the desert
B - 5. BIKE	E. When Stargirl cries, she does not shed tears, but this
I - 6. ROCK	F. Professor and friend to students
E - 7. LIGHT	G. Cinnamon was one
X - 8. BASKETBALL	H. For a person so different, Stargirl's house was ____
W - 9. CACTUS	I. MAHS basketball team massacred the Red ____ team
N -10. FILLER	J. Hot ____
C -11. STARGIRL	K. Team MAHS lost to in the playoffs
M -12. MARICOPAS	L. Silver contest award
T -13. FLOAT	M. The mountains
S -14. SPINELLI	N. Part of the newspaper Stargirl read
J -15. SEAT	O. Wayne's last name
O -16. PARR	P. Faculty adviser for Hot Seat
L -17. PLATE	Q. Porcupine ______
V -18. DORI	R. The Happy___held pebbles
U -19. BORLOCK	S. Author
D -20. ENCHANTED	T. Stargirl's bike and sidecar looked like a parade ____
Q -21. NECKTIE	U. Leo's last name
H -22. ORDINARY	V. Stargirl's 9th grade friend
K -23. GLENDALE	W. Senor Saguaro
R -24. WAGON	X. This MAHS team had a winning streak
Y -25. BUNNY	Y. Dance Stargirl led; ____ Hop

Stargirl Magic Squares 1

Match the definition with the vocabulary word. Put your answers in the magic squares below. When your answers are correct, all columns and rows will add to the same number.

A. PLATE
B. BUNNY
C. ROBINEAU
D. GREETING
E. CACTUS
F. RAT

G. TOMATO
H. UKULELE
I. EVELYN
J. LIGHT
K. ORDINARY
L. REGAL

M. FUNERAL
N. SUNFLOWER
O. PETER
P. MICA

1. Club requiring members to do nice things for others
2. Someone threw one in Stargirl's face
3. Word some parents used to describe Stargirl's appearance at the ball
4. Silver contest award
5. For a person so different, Stargirl's house was ___
6. Dance Stargirl led; ___ Hop
7. Stargirl went to Anna's grandfather's
8. Stargirl's instrument
9. Senor Saguaro
10. ____ Area High School
11. Faculty adviser for Hot Seat
12. When Stargirl cries, she does not shed tears, but this
13. Stargirl made her own ___ cards
14. Fictitious ordinary person: ___ Everybody
15. Cinnamon was one
16. Stargirl made a scrapbook for him

A=	B=	C=	D=
E=	F=	G=	H=
I=	J=	K=	L=
M=	N=	O=	P=

Stargirl Magic Squares 1 Answer Key

Match the definition with the vocabulary word. Put your answers in the magic squares below. When your answers are correct, all columns and rows will add to the same number.

A. PLATE
B. BUNNY
C. ROBINEAU
D. GREETING
E. CACTUS
F. RAT

G. TOMATO
H. UKULELE
I. EVELYN
J. LIGHT
K. ORDINARY
L. REGAL

M. FUNERAL
N. SUNFLOWER
O. PETER
P. MICA

1. Club requiring members to do nice things for others
2. Someone threw one in Stargirl's face
3. Word some parents used to describe Stargirl's appearance at the ball
4. Silver contest award
5. For a person so different, Stargirl's house was ___
6. Dance Stargirl led; ___ Hop
7. Stargirl went to Anna's grandfather's
8. Stargirl's instrument
9. Senor Saguaro
10. ____ Area High School
11. Faculty adviser for Hot Seat
12. When Stargirl cries, she does not shed tears, but this
13. Stargirl made her own ___ cards
14. Fictitious ordinary person: ___ Everybody
15. Cinnamon was one
16. Stargirl made a scrapbook for him

A=4	B=6	C=11	D=13
E=9	F=15	G=2	H=8
I=14	J=12	K=5	L=3
M=7	N=1	O=16	P=10

Stargirl Magic Squares 2

Match the definition with the vocabulary word. Put your answers in the magic squares below. When your answers are correct, all columns and rows will add to the same number.

A. ORATORICAL
B. PETER
C. WIN
D. SONORAN
E. MCSHANE
F. CHEERLEADER

G. MOVED
H. STARBOY
I. MOB
J. KOVAC
K. CHOOSE
L. FILLER

M. BORLOCK
N. DANNY
O. OCOTILLO
P. GOALPOST

1. Stargirl made a scrapbook for him
2. What Stargirl's family did after the ball
3. Leo had to ___ between Stargirl and his friends
4. He broke his leg in a bike accident
5. Leo's last name
6. Part of the newspaper Stargirl read
7. Leo
8. Kind of contest Stargirl entered

9. Stargirl climbed it at the football game
10. The Hot Seat jurors turned into a ___
11. Teacher who drove Susan and Leo to the state contest
12. The ___ desert
13. MAHS basketball team fans expected to ___
14. Stargirl was invited to become one
15. Sun Valley's injured star player
16. Ball where Stargirl regained her popularity

A=	B=	C=	D=
E=	F=	G=	H=
I=	J=	K=	L=
M=	N=	O=	P=

Stargirl Magic Squares 2 Answer Key

Match the definition with the vocabulary word. Put your answers in the magic squares
below. When your answers are correct, all columns and rows will add to the same
number.

A. ORATORICAL
B. PETER
C. WIN
D. SONORAN
E. MCSHANE
F. CHEERLEADER

G. MOVED
H. STARBOY
I. MOB
J. KOVAC
K. CHOOSE
L. FILLER

M. BORLOCK
N. DANNY
O. OCOTILLO
P. GOALPOST

1. Stargirl made a scrapbook for him
2. What Stargirl's family did after the ball
3. Leo had to ___ between Stargirl and his friends
4. He broke his leg in a bike accident
5. Leo's last name
6. Part of the newspaper Stargirl read
7. Leo
8. Kind of contest Stargirl entered

9. Stargirl climbed it at the football game
10. The Hot Seat jurors turned into a ___
11. Teacher who drove Susan and Leo to the state contest
12. The ___ desert
13. MAHS basketball team fans expected to ___
14. Stargirl was invited to become one
15. Sun Valley's injured star player
16. Ball where Stargirl regained her popularity

A=8	B=1	C=13	D=12
E=11	F=14	G=2	H=7
I=10	J=15	K=3	L=6
M=5	N=4	O=16	P=9

Stargirl Magic Squares 3

Match the definition with the vocabulary word. Put your answers in the magic squares below. When your answers are correct, all columns and rows will add to the same number.

A. CACTUS
B. ARCHIE
C. REGAL
D. BUNNY
E. DRIVER
F. FROGS

G. PLEDGE
H. DORI
I. GOALPOST
J. HERO
K. STALKING
L. CHOOSE

M. CHICKENS
N. FUNERAL
O. UKEE
P. STARGIRL

1. The students were like mud ___ awakening
2. Stargirl climbed it at the football game
3. ___ Dooks
4. Dance Stargirl led; ___ Hop
5. Don't count yours until they're hatched
6. Professor and friend to students
7. Stargirl's 9th grade friend
8. Leah thought Stargirl's card game was like ___

9. Word some parents used to describe Stargirl's appearance at the ball
10. Susan's alias
11. After the state oratorical contest, Susan expected to be welcomed back like one
12. Stargirl spent the 4th quarter of the Red Rock game outside talking to the bus ____
13. Leo had to ___ between Stargirl and his friends
14. Stargirl said an unusual ___ of Allegiance
15. Senor Saguaro
16. Stargirl went to Anna's grandfather's

A=	B=	C=	D=
E=	F=	G=	H=
I=	J=	K=	L=
M=	N=	O=	P=

Stargirl Magic Squares 3 Answer Key

Match the definition with the vocabulary word. Put your answers in the magic squares below. When your answers are correct, all columns and rows will add to the same number.

A. CACTUS
B. ARCHIE
C. REGAL
D. BUNNY
E. DRIVER
F. FROGS

G. PLEDGE
H. DORI
I. GOALPOST
J. HERO
K. STALKING
L. CHOOSE

M. CHICKENS
N. FUNERAL
O. UKEE
P. STARGIRL

1. The students were like mud ___ awakening
2. Stargirl climbed it at the football game
3. ___ Dooks
4. Dance Stargirl led; ___ Hop
5. Don't count yours until they're hatched
6. Professor and friend to students
7. Stargirl's 9th grade friend
8. Leah thought Stargirl's card game was like ___

9. Word some parents used to describe Stargirl's appearance at the ball
10. Susan's alias
11. After the state oratorical contest, Susan expected to be welcomed back like one
12. Stargirl spent the 4th quarter of the Red Rock game outside talking to the bus ____
13. Leo had to ___ between Stargirl and his friends
14. Stargirl said an unusual ___ of Allegiance
15. Senor Saguaro
16. Stargirl went to Anna's grandfather's

A=15	B=6	C=9	D=4
E=12	F=1	G=14	H=7
I=2	J=11	K=8	L=13
M=5	N=16	O=3	P=10

Stargirl Magic Squares 4

Match the definition with the vocabulary word. Put your answers in the magic squares below. When your answers are correct, all columns and rows will add to the same number.

A. SUNFLOWER
B. UKEE
C. BIKE
D. BORLOCK
E. UKULELE
F. HERO

G. HILLARI
H. FUNERAL
I. WAYNE
J. HEART
K. JURY
L. CHICO

M. SEAT
N. BARNEY
O. PETER
P. MCSHANE

1. Danny's new one went into the trash
2. Her eyes went straight to her ___
3. After the state oratorical contest, Susan expected to be welcomed back like one
4. Stargirl made a scrapbook for him
5. Teacher who drove Susan and Leo to the state contest
6. Stargirl's instrument
7. Hillari's boyfriend
8. Leo's last name
9. Hot ___
10. Stargirl went to Anna's grandfather's
11. Hand held camera and its operator for Hot Seat
12. Club requiring members to do nice things for others
13. ___ Dooks
14. Hot Seat panel asking questions
15. Miss Kimble; she dangled the rat
16. 60 million year old Paleocene rodent

A=	B=	C=	D=
E=	F=	G=	H=
I=	J=	K=	L=
M=	N=	O=	P=

Stargirl Magic Squares 4 Answer Key

Match the definition with the vocabulary word. Put your answers in the magic squares below. When your answers are correct, all columns and rows will add to the same number.

A. SUNFLOWER
B. UKEE
C. BIKE
D. BORLOCK
E. UKULELE
F. HERO

G. HILLARI
H. FUNERAL
I. WAYNE
J. HEART
K. JURY
L. CHICO

M. SEAT
N. BARNEY
O. PETER
P. MCSHANE

1. Danny's new one went into the trash
2. Her eyes went straight to her ___
3. After the state oratorical contest, Susan expected to be welcomed back like one
4. Stargirl made a scrapbook for him
5. Teacher who drove Susan and Leo to the state contest
6. Stargirl's instrument
7. Hillari's boyfriend
8. Leo's last name
9. Hot ___
10. Stargirl went to Anna's grandfather's
11. Hand held camera and its operator for Hot Seat
12. Club requiring members to do nice things for others
13. ___ Dooks
14. Hot Seat panel asking questions
15. Miss Kimble; she dangled the rat
16. 60 million year old Paleocene rodent

A=12	B=13	C=1	D=8
E=6	F=3	G=15	H=10
I=7	J=2	K=14	L=11
M=9	N=16	O=4	P=5

Stargirl Word Search 1

```
M  I  C  A  K  N  A  R  C  H  I  E  W  C  A  V  O  K  A  Y
W  U  F  M  Y  E  O  E  A  W  B  Q  X  Y  A  E  B  O  M  R
I  S  D  L  C  B  V  K  S  Y  O  H  D  R  T  R  M  R  G  F
N  X  E  P  I  S  E  I  L  W  M  S  V  A  E  G  D  E  L  P
L  V  M  N  I  L  H  B  N  A  V  O  L  N  N  G  N  W  I  F
E  V  E  V  E  E  B  A  K  Y  B  P  N  I  W  N  A  O  G  F
L  A  Z  L  R  S  U  P  N  N  D  F  T  D  F  T  Y  L  H  W
U  S  U  O  Y  O  N  M  P  E  T  E  R  R  O  Y  R  F  T  V
X  K  T  T  E  O  N  D  C  W  E  V  O  O  R  R  F  N  B  N
U  R  Z  A  N  H  Y  R  L  R  X  G  Z  U  A  H  I  U  T  H
T  K  G  M  R  C  L  I  G  B  S  R  J  P  E  E  X  S  O  F
S  Y  L  O  A  G  B  V  S  C  N  O  Y  I  E  A  R  B  O  B
O  O  E  T  B  R  I  E  A  H  Q  C  T  P  G  R  C  S  L  C
P  B  N  F  U  N  E  R  A  L  U  K  E  E  N  T  A  E  S  R
L  R  D  O  Q  T  A  O  L  F  C  N  O  G  A  W  C  N  H  V
A  A  A  Z  R  W  H  S  T  E  S  M  N  R  H  S  T  S  E  W
O  T  L  M  A  A  B  O  N  E  G  R  F  E  C  Q  U  E  D  M
G  S  E  Y  L  U  N  C  H  M  O  V  E  D  D  J  S  S  S  Q
```

60 million year old Paleocene rodent (6)
After the state oratorical contest, Susan expected to be welcomed back like one (4)
Another Susan alias (6)
Archie's ___ was Stargirl's office (8)
Cinnamon was one (3)
Club requiring members to do nice things for others (9)
Dance Stargirl led; ___ Hop (5)
Danny's new one went into the trash (4)
Faculty adviser for Hot Seat (8)
Fictitious ordinary person: ___ Everybody (6)
First to dance with Stargirl (7)
For a person so different, Stargirl's house was ___ (8)
He broke his leg in a bike accident (5)
Her eyes went straight to her ___ (5)
Hillari's boyfriend (5)
Hot Seat anchor (5)
Hot Seat panel asking questions (4)
Hot ___ (4)
Large, extinct bird (3)
Leo (7)
Leo had to ___ between Stargirl and his friends (6)
Leo wanted Stargirl to do this (6)
Leo's Valentine ___ said: I love you (4)
Loyal Order of the Stone ____ (4)
MAHS basketball team fans expected to ___ (3)
MAHS basketball team massacred the Red ___ team (4)
Porcupine _____ (7)
Professor and friend to students (6)
Senor Saguaro (6)
Silver contest award (5)
Someone threw one in Stargirl's face (6)
Sometimes we need to erase them (6)
Stargirl climbed it at the football game (8)
Stargirl made a scrapbook for him (5)
Stargirl made her own ___ cards (8)
Stargirl said an unusual ___ of Allegiance (6)
Stargirl spent the 4th quarter of the Red Rock game outside talking to the bus ____ (6)
Stargirl went to Anna's grandfather's (7)
Stargirl's 9th grade friend (4)
Stargirl's bike and sidecar looked like a parade ___ (5)
Stargirl's instrument (7)
Stargirl's last name (7)
Sun Valley's injured star player (5)
Susan's alias (8)
Teacher who drove Susan and Leo to the state contest (7)
Team MAHS lost to in the playoffs (8)
The Happy___held pebbles (5)
The Hot Seat jurors turned into a ___ (3)
The ___ desert (7)
The students did this to Stargirl and Leo (7)
The students were like mud ___ awakening (5)
Time when Stargirl sang Happy Birthday (5)
Wayne's last name (4)
What Stargirl's family did after the ball (5)
When Stargirl cries, she does not shed tears, but this (5)
Word some parents used to describe Stargirl's appearance at the ball (5)
___ Dooks (4)
____ Area High School (4)

Stargirl Word Search 1 Answer Key

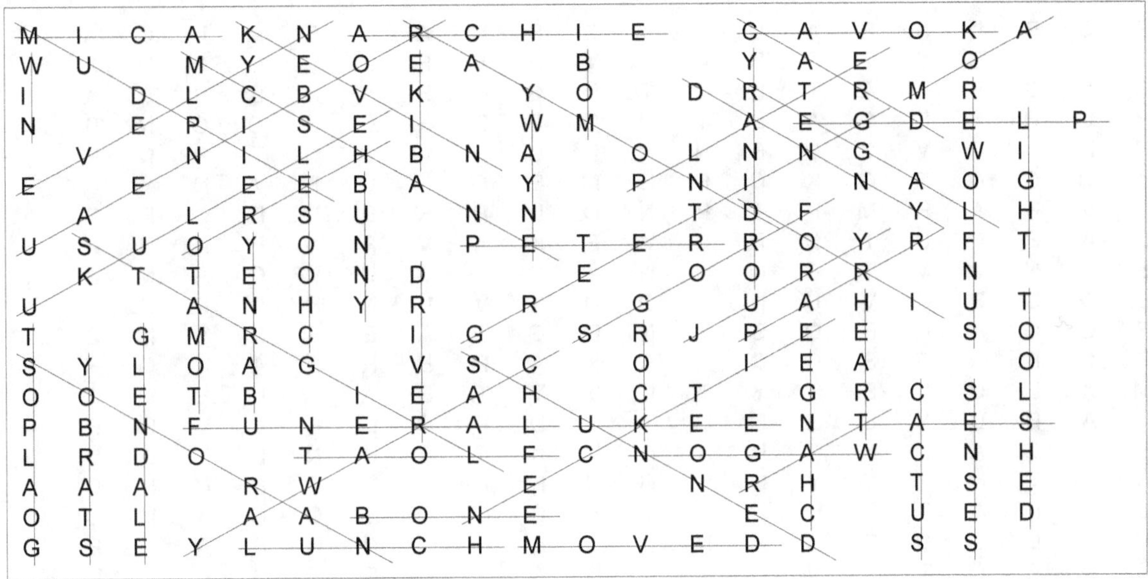

60 million year old Paleocene rodent (6)
After the state oratorical contest, Susan expected to be welcomed back like one (4)
Another Susan alias (6)
Archie's ___ was Stargirl's office (8)
Cinnamon was one (3)
Club requiring members to do nice things for others (9)
Dance Stargirl led; ___ Hop (5)
Danny's new one went into the trash (4)
Faculty adviser for Hot Seat (8)
Fictitious ordinary person: ___ Everybody (6)
First to dance with Stargirl (7)
For a person so different, Stargirl's house was ___ (8)
He broke his leg in a bike accident (5)
Her eyes went straight to her ___ (5)
Hillari's boyfriend (5)
Hot Seat anchor (5)
Hot Seat panel asking questions (4)
Hot ___ (4)
Large, extinct bird (3)
Leo (7)
Leo had to ___ between Stargirl and his friends (6)
Leo wanted Stargirl to do this (6)
Leo's Valentine ____said: I love you (4)
Loyal Order of the Stone ____ (4)
MAHS basketball team fans expected to ___ (3)
MAHS basketball team massacred the Red ___ team (4)
Porcupine _____ (7)
Professor and friend to students (6)
Senor Saguaro (6)
Silver contest award (5)

Someone threw one in Stargirl's face (6)
Sometimes we need to erase them (6)
Stargirl climbed it at the football game (8)
Stargirl made a scrapbook for him (5)
Stargirl made her own ___ cards (8)
Stargirl said an unusual ___ of Allegiance (6)
Stargirl spent the 4th quarter of the Red Rock game outside talking to the bus ____ (6)
Stargirl went to Anna's grandfather's (7)
Stargirl's 9th grade friend (4)
Stargirl's bike and sidecar looked like a parade ___ (5)
Stargirl's instrument (7)
Stargirl's last name (7)
Sun Valley's injured star player (5)
Susan's alias (8)
Teacher who drove Susan and Leo to the state contest (7)
Team MAHS lost to in the playoffs (8)
The Happy___held pebbles (5)
The Hot Seat jurors turned into a ___ (3)
The ___ desert (7)
The students did this to Stargirl and Leo (7)
The students were like mud ___ awakening (5)
Time when Stargirl sang Happy Birthday (5)
Wayne's last name (4)
What Stargirl's family did after the ball (5)
When Stargirl cries, she does not shed tears, but this (5)
Word some parents used to describe Stargirl's appearance at the ball (5)
___ Dooks (4)
____ Area High School (4)

```
R O B I N E A U L M C S H A N E M I C A
R O J S Y T S R W U V H S E I N O O D X
A X C P L A T E C T N G A P A R B S A K
P L H K E S A L J H O C D N E R O O N B
U K I C V V L E N R I U H W G N T R N M
K O C G E G K C F E M E O R O E W D Y D
U V K A H M I T R N C L R R E L L I F S
L A E F C T N R R W F K A V F X F N R F
E C N W M T G O H N J N T Q U W O A M E
L D S R C V U N U O U K V I N R I R N Y
E G O A L P O S T N R G T A E S R Y M Z
P C B R G S C Q T E Y A P H R F A K O H
M X L U I E J Y T L V Y T B A W L E V J
C A R D N S E E W T Q D P O L I L V E P
R E G A L N P P A B I K E R R N I I D L
H V T M R E Y O G G N E N L X I H N S D
D D L A D S L L O S K C O O Z O C I H C
M S B J Q F C X N U Q B B C N R B A L B
G R E E T I N G T S B A S K E T B A L L
```

60 million year old Paleocene rodent (6)

After the state oratorical contest, Susan expected to be welcomed back like one (4)

Another Susan alias (6)

Cinnamon was one (3)

Club requiring members to do nice things for others (9)

Dance Stargirl led; ___ Hop (5)

Danny's new one went into the trash (4)

Don't count yours until they're hatched (8)

Faculty adviser for Hot Seat (8)

Fictitious ordinary person: ___ Everybody (6)

For a person so different, Stargirl's house was ___ (8)

Hand held camera and its operator for Hot Seat (5)

He broke his leg in a bike accident (5)

Her eyes went straight to her ___ (5)

Hillari's boyfriend (5)

Hot Seat anchor (5)

Hot Seat panel asking questions (4)

Hot ___ (4)

Kind of contest Stargirl entered (10)

Large, extinct bird (3)

Leah thought Stargirl's card game was like ___ (8)

Leo wanted Stargirl to do this (6)

Leo's Valentine ____ said: I love you (4)

Leo's last name (7)

Loyal Order of the Stone ____ (4)

MAHS basketball team fans expected to ___ (3)

MAHS basketball team massacred the Red ___ team (4)

Miss Kimble; she dangled the rat (7)

Name of MAHS sports teams (9)

Part of the newspaper Stargirl read (6)

Porcupine ______ (7)

Professor and friend to students (6)

Senor Saguaro (6)

Silver contest award (5)

Sometimes we need to erase them (6)

Stargirl climbed it at the football game (8)

Stargirl made a scrapbook for him (5)

Stargirl made her own ___ cards (8)

Stargirl went to Anna's grandfather's (7)

Stargirl's 9th grade friend (4)

Stargirl's bike and sidecar looked like a parade ___ (5)

Stargirl's instrument (7)

Sun Valley's injured star player (5)

Teacher who drove Susan and Leo to the state contest (7)

The Happy___held pebbles (5)

The Hot Seat jurors turned into a ___ (3)

The ___ desert (7)

The students were like mud ___ awakening (5)

This MAHS team had a winning streak (10)

Time when Stargirl sang Happy Birthday (5)

Wayne's last name (4)

What Stargirl's family did after the ball (5)

When Stargirl cries, she does not shed tears, but this (5)

Word some parents used to describe Stargirl's appearance at the ball (5)

___ Dooks (4)

____ Area High School (4)

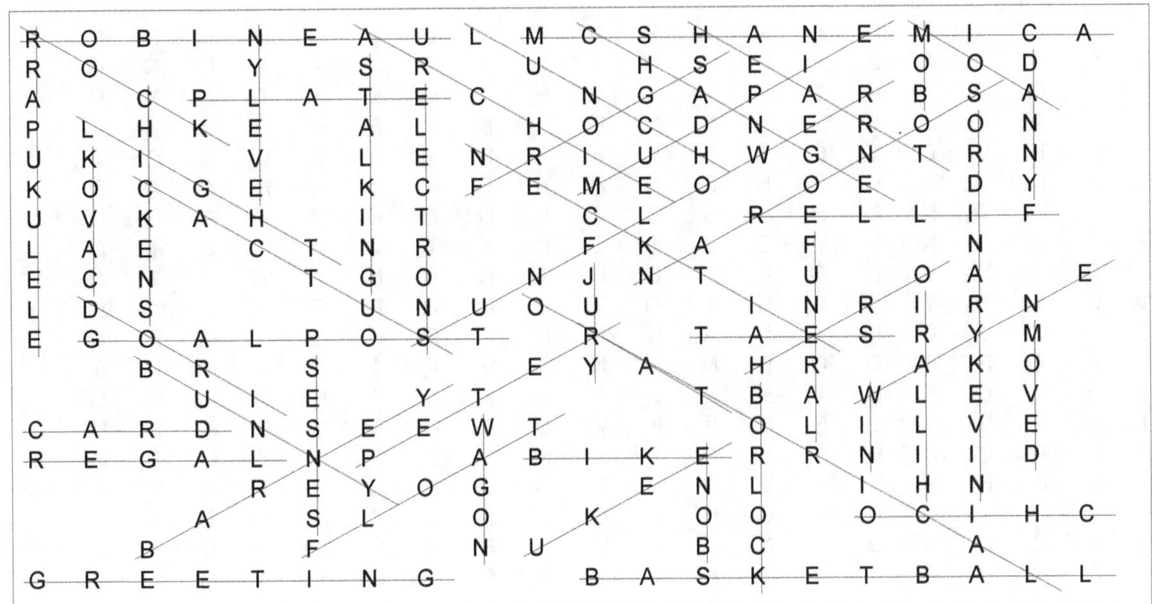

60 million year old Paleocene rodent (6)

After the state oratorical contest, Susan expected to be welcomed back like one (4)

Another Susan alias (6)

Cinnamon was one (3)

Club requiring members to do nice things for others (9)

Dance Stargirl led; ___ Hop (5)

Danny's new one went into the trash (4)

Don't count yours until they're hatched (8)

Faculty adviser for Hot Seat (8)

Fictitious ordinary person: ___ Everybody (6)

For a person so different, Stargirl's house was ___ (8)

Hand held camera and its operator for Hot Seat (5)

He broke his leg in a bike accident (5)

Her eyes went straight to her ___ (5)

Hillari's boyfriend (5)

Hot Seat anchor (5)

Hot Seat panel asking questions (4)

Hot ___ (4)

Kind of contest Stargirl entered (10)

Large, extinct bird (3)

Leah thought Stargirl's card game was like ___ (8)

Leo wanted Stargirl to do this (6)

Leo's Valentine ____ said: I love you (4)

Leo's last name (7)

Loyal Order of the Stone ____ (4)

MAHS basketball team fans expected to ___ (3)

MAHS basketball team massacred the Red ___ team (4)

Miss Kimble; she dangled the rat (7)

Name of MAHS sports teams (9)

Part of the newspaper Stargirl read (6)

Porcupine _____ (7)

Professor and friend to students (6)

Senor Saguaro (6)

Silver contest award (5)

Sometimes we need to erase them (6)

Stargirl climbed it at the football game (8)

Stargirl made a scrapbook for him (5)

Stargirl made her own ___ cards (8)

Stargirl went to Anna's grandfather's (7)

Stargirl's 9th grade friend (4)

Stargirl's bike and sidecar looked like a parade ___ (5)

Stargirl's instrument (7)

Sun Valley's injured star player (5)

Teacher who drove Susan and Leo to the state contest (7)

The Happy___ held pebbles (5)

The Hot Seat jurors turned into a ___ (3)

The ___ desert (7)

The students were like mud ___ awakening (5)

This MAHS team had a winning streak (10)

Time when Stargirl sang Happy Birthday (5)

Wayne's last name (4)

What Stargirl's family did after the ball (5)

When Stargirl cries, she does not shed tears, but this (5)

Word some parents used to describe Stargirl's appearance at the ball (5)

___ Dooks (4)

____ Area High School (4)

```
C S E N C H A N T E D F I L L E N I P S
A O P E T E R E S D C U K E E N T R R G
C N M Q X K T C E R M N T O M A T O Y P
T O T A E S J K N I P E B H B H P D K V
U R H V D V E T S V A R E W K S C B C Y
S A I Q A G Y I E E R A E I E C R A O Z
K N L U N C H E S R R L D N O M Y A R Q
O F M A N L W O E T E B Y T O R I E T D
V P H W Y L O L Z C M A O C M Y W C T Q
A C Y O Y H L K T O W B K R P O S J A K
C M U V C I I R A L L I H P L E D G E H
S A A R F O O P M Q N K V F A O Y N H S
H R E G E N T K M G J E N L T K C I E G
U I N V S G F I B K W U T D E L E K R M
N C I C E H A I L A S M U D P I E L O B
N O B H N L R L G L Y O W H H G J A Y K
E P O I O D Y O L T O B D C Z H U T J T
D A R C B U N N Y A W A R A C T R S R Z
K S G O R F L O A T B A R N E Y Y M P Q
```

ARCHIE	ELECTRONS	MARICOPAS	REGAL
BARNEY	ENCHANTED	MCSHANE	ROBINEAU
BIKE	EVELYN	MICA	ROCK
BONE	FILLER	MOA	SEAT
BORLOCK	FLOAT	MOB	SENSES
BUNNY	FROGS	MOCKINGBIRD	SHUNNED
CACTUS	FUNERAL	MUDPIE	SONORAN
CARAWAY	HEART	NECKTIE	SPINELLI
CARD	HERO	OCOTILLO	STALKING
CHANGE	HILLARI	PARR	SUNFLOWER
CHICO	JURY	PETER	TOMATO
CHOOSE	KEVIN	PLATE	UKEE
DANNY	KOVAC	PLEDGE	WAGON
DORI	LIGHT	RAT	WAYNE
DRIVER	LUNCH	RAYMOND	WIN

Stargirl Word Search 3 Answer Key

```
C S E N C H A N T E D F I L L E N I P S
A O P E T E R E S D U K E E N R
C N K C E N R I N T O M A T O
T O T A E S K N I P E H H D K
U R V D E T S V A R W H S C R A C
S A I A G I E R A E I E C R A O
K N L U N C H E S R L D N O M Y A R T D
O A N O E T E B Y O I E
V H Y O L L C M A O C W C
A C O H L T O W B K R P O A
C M U C I R A L L I H P L E D G E
S A R F O O N K F A O N H
H R E E N T G E N T C I E R
U I N V S G I B W U E L K O
N C I C E A I L A S M U D P I E
N O B H N L R L G L O H G J A
E P O I O D Y O O B C H T T
D A R C B U N N Y A W A R A C T U R S
S G O R F L O A T B A R N E Y Y
```

ARCHIE	ELECTRONS	MARICOPAS	REGAL
BARNEY	ENCHANTED	MCSHANE	ROBINEAU
BIKE	EVELYN	MICA	ROCK
BONE	FILLER	MOA	SEAT
BORLOCK	FLOAT	MOB	SENSES
BUNNY	FROGS	MOCKINGBIRD	SHUNNED
CACTUS	FUNERAL	MUDPIE	SONORAN
CARAWAY	HEART	NECKTIE	SPINELLI
CARD	HERO	OCOTILLO	STALKING
CHANGE	HILLARI	PARR	SUNFLOWER
CHICO	JURY	PETER	TOMATO
CHOOSE	KEVIN	PLATE	UKEE
DANNY	KOVAC	PLEDGE	WAGON
DORI	LIGHT	RAT	WAYNE
DRIVER	LUNCH	RAYMOND	WIN

Stargirl Word Search 4

```
M  L  S  F  Y  K  X  W  X  X  B  C  A  R  A  W  A  Y  D  K
X  A  T  B  P  C  K  S  A  Y  A  L  S  C  J  R  S  N  O  K
K  C  A  L  O  O  R  E  Y  Y  R  U  I  R  E  N  J  Y  R  L
F  I  L  L  E  R  W  A  G  O  N  M  O  V  E  D  E  W  I  N
G  R  K  Y  A  Z  L  T  C  F  E  E  I  K  T  L  I  G  L  G
Y  O  I  P  X  J  X  O  L  R  Y  R  C  F  A  D  H  F  L  T
R  T  N  H  C  F  U  O  C  N  D  I  Y  D  L  T  C  D  E  Q
L  A  G  E  R  H  W  R  Q  K  H  Q  N  P  P  F  R  D  N  G
S  R  T  V  C  E  I  N  Y  C  C  E  N  X  W  I  A  M  I  G
T  O  P  N  R  W  Z  C  V  M  L  N  A  X  B  H  J  Q  P  G
A  P  U  C  G  Y  K  U  O  G  O  O  D  G  D  E  D  O  S  Y
R  L  T  A  O  L  F  K  E  K  I  B  N  E  O  R  C  D  R  V
B  E  O  C  A  R  N  E  O  Z  S  I  T  T  A  O  E  E  O  L
O  D  O  T  L  I  E  E  S  V  K  N  A  C  T  N  T  G  B  V
Y  G  L  U  P  G  C  D  X  C  A  M  Y  I  N  E  K  N  I  T
V  E  S  S  O  R  K  P  O  H  O  C  L  U  P  M  O  A  N  H
W  K  H  K  S  A  T  M  C  T  K  L  H  E  A  R  T  H  E  M
F  G  E  P  T  T  I  N  L  F  O  S  G  O  R  F  X  C  A  Z
V  Q  D  L  L  S  E  G  H  M  C  S  H  A  N  E  M  M  U  X
```

ARCHIE	ENCHANTED	MOA	ROCK
BARNEY	FILLER	MOB	SEAT
BIKE	FLOAT	MOCKINGBIRD	SHUNNED
BONE	FROGS	MOVED	SPINELLI
BORLOCK	GLENDALE	NECKTIE	STALKING
CACTUS	GOALPOST	OCOTILLO	STARBOY
CARAWAY	HEART	ORATORICAL	STARGIRL
CARD	HERO	PARR	SUNFLOWER
CHANGE	JURY	PETER	TOMATO
CHICKENS	KOVAC	PLATE	TOOLSHED
CHICO	LIGHT	PLEDGE	UKEE
DANNY	LUNCH	RAT	WAGON
DORI	MCSHANE	REGAL	WAYNE
DRIVER	MICA	ROBINEAU	WIN

Stargirl Word Search 4 Answer Key

ARCHIE	ENCHANTED	MOA	ROCK
BARNEY	FILLER	MOB	SEAT
BIKE	FLOAT	MOCKINGBIRD	SHUNNED
BONE	FROGS	MOVED	SPINELLI
BORLOCK	GLENDALE	NECKTIE	STALKING
CACTUS	GOALPOST	OCOTILLO	STARBOY
CARAWAY	HEART	ORATORICAL	STARGIRL
CARD	HERO	PARR	SUNFLOWER
CHANGE	JURY	PETER	TOMATO
CHICKENS	KOVAC	PLATE	TOOLSHED
CHICO	LIGHT	PLEDGE	UKEE
DANNY	LUNCH	RAT	WAGON
DORI	MCSHANE	REGAL	WAYNE
DRIVER	MICA	ROBINEAU	WIN

Stargirl Crossword 1

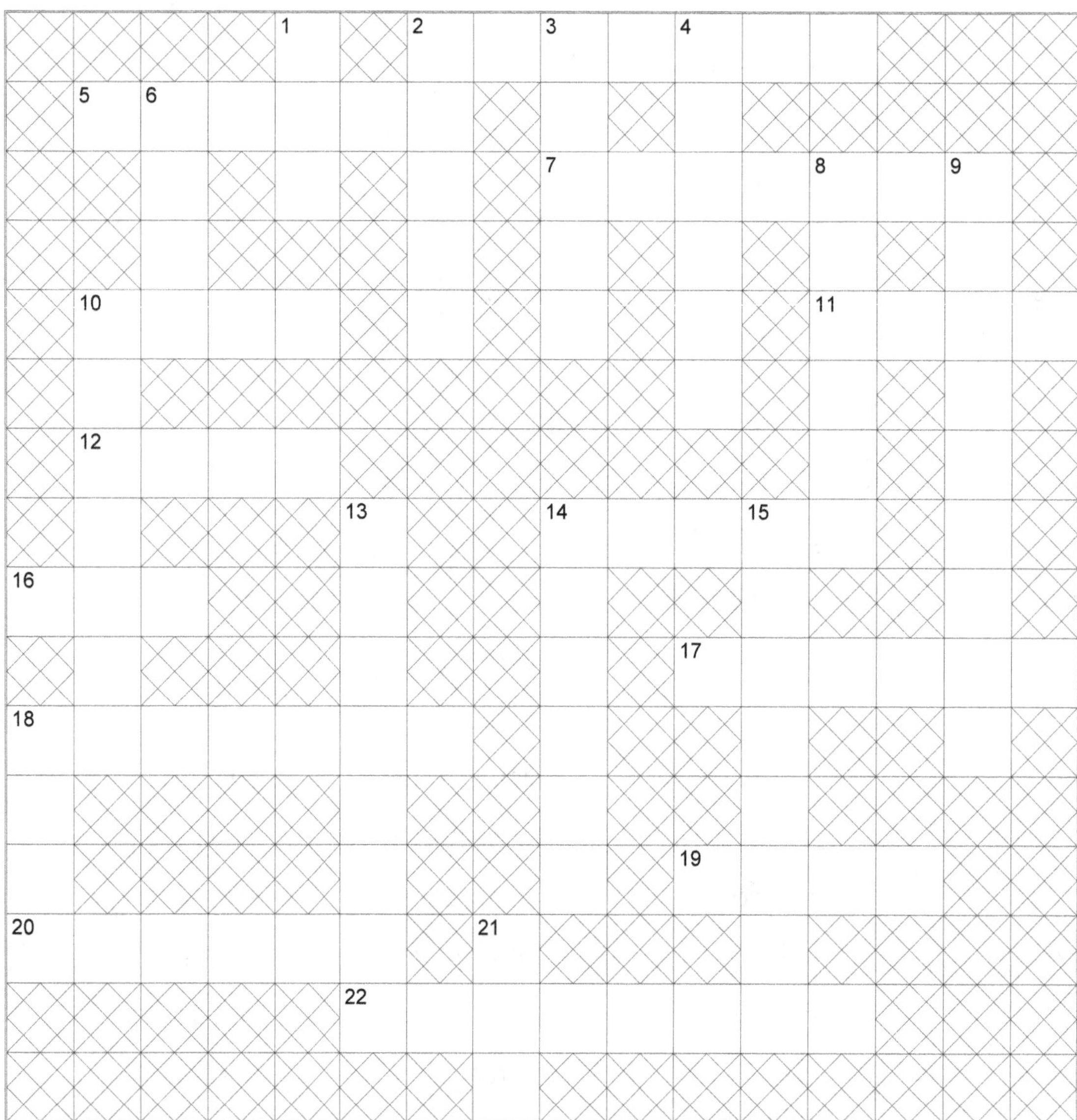

Across

2. Miss Kimble; she dangled the rat
5. Leo had to ___ between Stargirl and his friends
7. Porcupine _____
10. Loyal Order of the Stone ____
11. ____ Area High School
12. MAHS basketball team massacred the Red ___ team
14. Hand held camera and its operator for Hot Seat
16. The Hot Seat jurors turned into a ___
17. Part of the newspaper Stargirl read
18. Stargirl's instrument
19. Hot ___
20. Fictitious ordinary person: ___ Everybody
22. Stargirl climbed it at the football game

Down

1. Large, extinct bird
2. Her eyes went straight to her ___
3. Time when Stargirl sang Happy Birthday
4. Professor and friend to students
6. After the state oratorical contest, Susan expected to be welcomed back like one
8. Someone threw one in Stargirl's face
9. Stargirl showed Leo an ____ place in the desert
10. Leo's last name
13. Leah thought Stargirl's card game was like ___
14. Senor Saguaro
15. Don't count yours until they're hatched
18. ___ Dooks
21. Cinnamon was one

Stargirl Crossword 1 Answer Key

<table>
<tr><td></td><td></td><td></td><td></td><td>1
M</td><td></td><td>2
H</td><td>I</td><td>3
L</td><td>L</td><td>4
A</td><td>R</td><td>I</td><td></td><td></td><td></td></tr>
<tr><td></td><td>5
C</td><td>6
H</td><td>O</td><td>O</td><td>S</td><td>E</td><td></td><td>U</td><td></td><td>R</td><td></td><td></td><td></td><td></td><td></td></tr>
<tr><td></td><td></td><td>E</td><td></td><td>A</td><td></td><td>A</td><td></td><td>7
N</td><td>E</td><td>C</td><td>K</td><td>8
T</td><td>I</td><td>9
E</td><td></td></tr>
<tr><td></td><td></td><td>R</td><td></td><td></td><td></td><td>R</td><td></td><td>C</td><td></td><td>H</td><td></td><td>O</td><td></td><td>N</td><td></td></tr>
<tr><td></td><td>10
B</td><td>O</td><td>N</td><td>E</td><td></td><td>T</td><td></td><td>H</td><td></td><td>I</td><td></td><td>11
M</td><td>I</td><td>C</td><td>A</td></tr>
<tr><td></td><td>O</td><td></td><td></td><td></td><td></td><td></td><td></td><td></td><td></td><td>E</td><td></td><td>A</td><td></td><td>H</td><td></td></tr>
<tr><td></td><td>12
R</td><td>O</td><td>C</td><td>K</td><td></td><td></td><td></td><td></td><td></td><td></td><td></td><td>T</td><td></td><td>A</td><td></td></tr>
<tr><td></td><td>L</td><td></td><td></td><td></td><td>13
S</td><td></td><td></td><td>14
C</td><td>H</td><td>I</td><td>15
C</td><td>O</td><td></td><td>N</td><td></td></tr>
<tr><td>16
M</td><td>O</td><td>B</td><td></td><td></td><td>T</td><td></td><td></td><td>A</td><td></td><td></td><td>H</td><td></td><td></td><td>T</td><td></td></tr>
<tr><td></td><td>C</td><td></td><td></td><td></td><td>A</td><td></td><td></td><td>C</td><td></td><td>17
F</td><td>I</td><td>L</td><td>L</td><td>E</td><td>R</td></tr>
<tr><td>18
U</td><td>K</td><td>U</td><td>L</td><td>E</td><td>L</td><td>E</td><td></td><td>T</td><td></td><td></td><td>C</td><td></td><td></td><td>D</td><td></td></tr>
<tr><td>K</td><td></td><td></td><td></td><td></td><td>K</td><td></td><td></td><td>U</td><td></td><td></td><td>K</td><td></td><td></td><td></td><td></td></tr>
<tr><td>E</td><td></td><td></td><td></td><td></td><td>I</td><td></td><td></td><td>S</td><td></td><td>19
S</td><td>E</td><td>A</td><td>T</td><td></td><td></td></tr>
<tr><td>20
E</td><td>V</td><td>E</td><td>L</td><td>Y</td><td>N</td><td></td><td>21
R</td><td></td><td></td><td></td><td>N</td><td></td><td></td><td></td><td></td></tr>
<tr><td></td><td></td><td></td><td></td><td></td><td>22
G</td><td>O</td><td>A</td><td>L</td><td>P</td><td>O</td><td>S</td><td>T</td><td></td><td></td><td></td></tr>
<tr><td></td><td></td><td></td><td></td><td></td><td></td><td></td><td>T</td><td></td><td></td><td></td><td></td><td></td><td></td><td></td><td></td></tr>
</table>

Across
2. Miss Kimble; she dangled the rat
5. Leo had to ___ between Stargirl and his friends
7. Porcupine _____
10. Loyal Order of the Stone ____
11. ____ Area High School
12. MAHS basketball team massacred the Red ___ team
14. Hand held camera and its operator for Hot Seat
16. The Hot Seat jurors turned into a ___
17. Part of the newspaper Stargirl read
18. Stargirl's instrument
19. Hot ___
20. Fictitious ordinary person: ___ Everybody
22. Stargirl climbed it at the football game

Down
1. Large, extinct bird
2. Her eyes went straight to her ___
3. Time when Stargirl sang Happy Birthday
4. Professor and friend to students
6. After the state oratorical contest, Susan expected to be welcomed back like one
8. Someone threw one in Stargirl's face
9. Stargirl showed Leo an ____ place in the desert
10. Leo's last name
13. Leah thought Stargirl's card game was like ___
14. Senor Saguaro
15. Don't count yours until they're hatched
18. ___ Dooks
21. Cinnamon was one

Stargirl Crossword 2

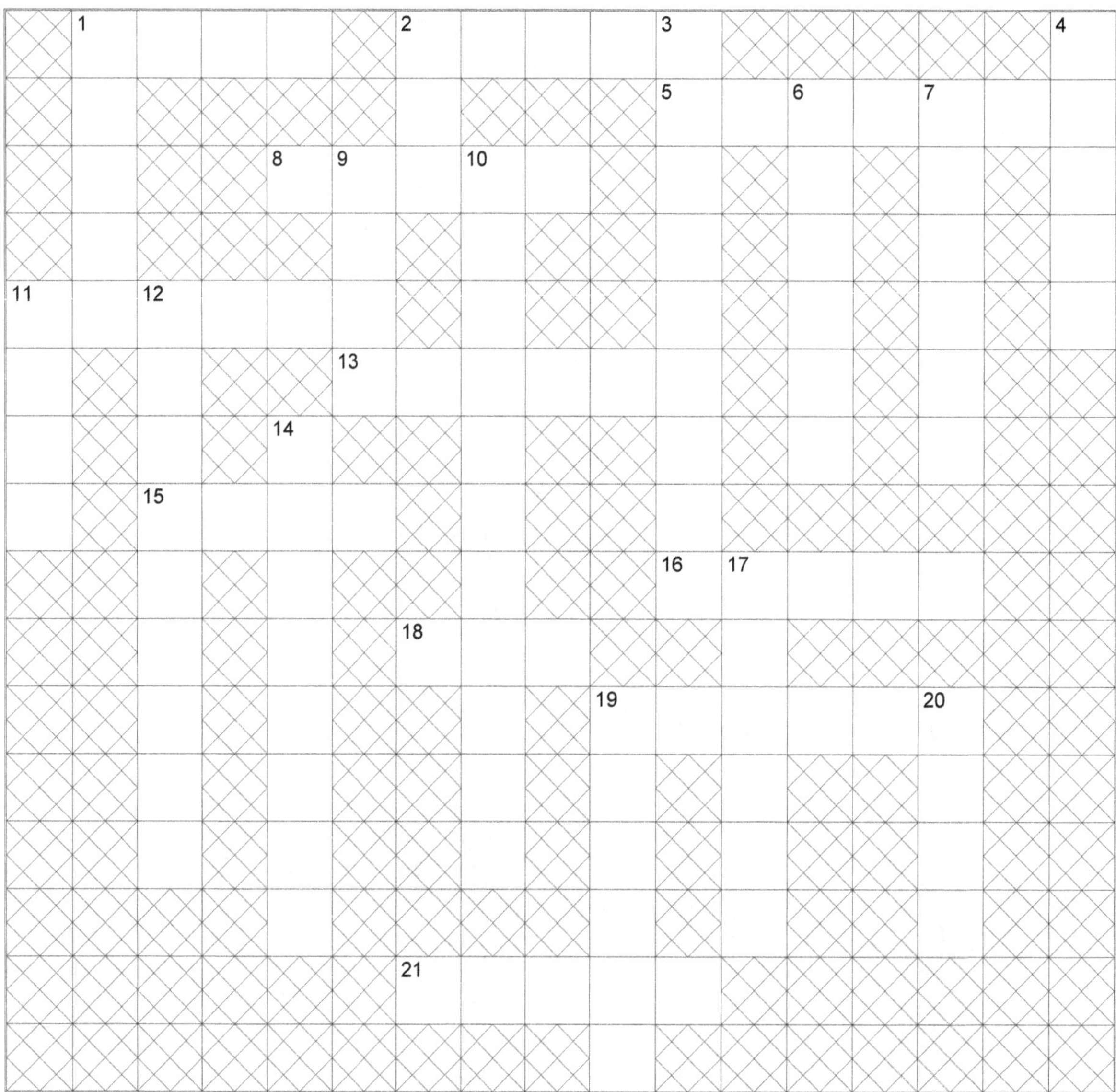

Across
1. MAHS basketball team massacred the Red ___ team
2. Hillari's boyfriend
5. Porcupine _____
8. Time when Stargirl sang Happy Birthday
11. Stargirl said an unusual ___ of Allegiance
13. Fictitious ordinary person: ___ Everybody
15. Leo's Valentine ____ said: I love you
16. He broke his leg in a bike accident
18. Cinnamon was one
19. Senor Saguaro
21. The students were like mud ___ awakening

Down
1. Word some parents used to describe Stargirl's appearance at the ball
2. MAHS basketball team fans expected to ___
3. Stargirl showed Leo an ____ place in the desert
4. Her eyes went straight to her ___
6. Leo had to ___ between Stargirl and his friends
7. Someone threw one in Stargirl's face
9. ___ Dooks
10. Stargirl was invited to become one
11. Wayne's last name
12. Name of MAHS sports teams
14. For a person so different, Stargirl's house was ___
17. Professor and friend to students
19. Leo wanted Stargirl to do this
20. Hot ___

Stargirl Crossword 2 Answer Key

	1 R	O	C	K		2 W	A	Y	N	3 E							4 H
	E					I				5 N	E	6 C	K	7 T	I	E
	G		8 L	9 U	N	10 C	H		C		H		O		A
	A			K		H			H		O		M		R
11 P	L	12 E	D	G	E		E		A		O		A		T
A		L			13 E	V	E	L	Y	N		S		T
R		E		14 O		R		T		E		O
R		15 C	A	R	D		L		E
		T		D		E		16 D	17 A	N	N	Y
		R		I		18 R	A	T		R
		O		N		D		19 C	A	C	T	20 U	S
		N		A		E		H		H		E
		S		R		R		A		I		A
				Y				N		16 E		T
					21 F	R	O	G	S
								E

Across
1. MAHS basketball team massacred the Red ___ team
2. Hillari's boyfriend
5. Porcupine _____
8. Time when Stargirl sang Happy Birthday
11. Stargirl said an unusual ___ of Allegiance
13. Fictitious ordinary person: ___ Everybody
15. Leo's Valentine ____ said: I love you
16. He broke his leg in a bike accident
18. Cinnamon was one
19. Senor Saguaro
21. The students were like mud ___ awakening

Down
1. Word some parents used to describe Stargirl's appearance at the ball
2. MAHS basketball team fans expected to ___
3. Stargirl showed Leo an ____ place in the desert
4. Her eyes went straight to her ___
6. Leo had to ___ between Stargirl and his friends
7. Someone threw one in Stargirl's face
9. ___ Dooks
10. Stargirl was invited to become one
11. Wayne's last name
12. Name of MAHS sports teams
14. For a person so different, Stargirl's house was ___
17. Professor and friend to students
19. Leo wanted Stargirl to do this
20. Hot ___

Stargirl Crossword 3

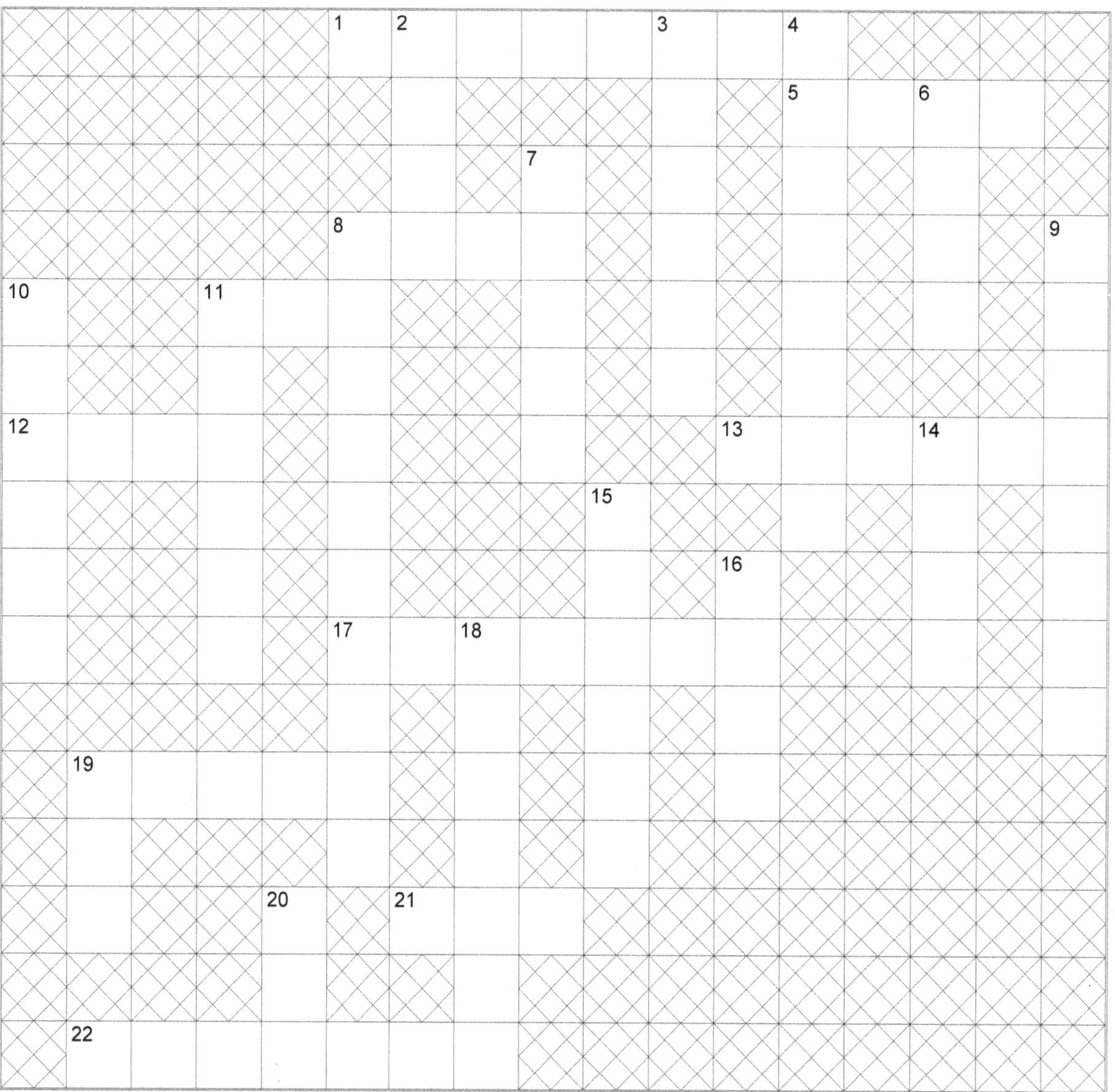

Across

1. Don't count yours until they're hatched
5. Wayne's last name
8. Loyal Order of the Stone ____
11. Large, extinct bird
12. Leo's Valentine ____ said: I love you
13. Stargirl said an unusual ___ of Allegiance
17. Leo's last name
19. Word some parents used to describe Stargirl's appearance at the ball
21. The Hot Seat jurors turned into a ___
22. The students did this to Stargirl and Leo

Down

2. After the state oratorical contest, Susan expected to be welcomed back like one
3. Fictitious ordinary person: ___ Everybody
4. Author
6. MAHS basketball team massacred the Red ___ team
7. Her eyes went straight to her ___
8. This MAHS team had a winning streak
9. Stargirl made her own ___ cards
10. Senor Saguaro
11. Another Susan alias
14. Stargirl's 9th grade friend
15. Leo had to ___ between Stargirl and his friends
16. ___ Dooks
18. First to dance with Stargirl
19. Cinnamon was one
20. MAHS basketball team fans expected to ___

Stargirl Crossword 3 Answer Key

				1 C	2 H	I	C	K	E	N	S			
				E				V		5 P	A	R	6 R	R
				R		7 H	E		I		O			
			8 B	O	N	E	L		N		C		9 G	
10 C		11 M	O	A		A	Y		E	K	R			
A		U	S		R	N		L		E			
12 C	A	R	D		T		13 P	L	E	14 D	G	E
T		P	E			15 C		I		O	T	
U		I	T		H	16 U	R	I			
S		E	17 B	O	18 R	L	O	C	K	I	N
		A	A		O	E	G			
19 R	E	G	A	L	Y	S	E			
A	L	M	E			
T	20 W	21 M	O	B			
I	N			
22 S	H	U	N	N	E	D

Across

1. Don't count yours until they're hatched
5. Wayne's last name
8. Loyal Order of the Stone ____
11. Large, extinct bird
12. Leo's Valentine ____ said: I love you
13. Stargirl said an unusual ___ of Allegiance
17. Leo's last name
19. Word some parents used to describe Stargirl's appearance at the ball
21. The Hot Seat jurors turned into a ___
22. The students did this to Stargirl and Leo

Down

2. After the state oratorical contest, Susan expected to be welcomed back like one
3. Fictitious ordinary person: ___ Everybody
4. Author
6. MAHS basketball team massacred the Red ___ team
7. Her eyes went straight to her ___
8. This MAHS team had a winning streak
9. Stargirl made her own ___ cards
10. Senor Saguaro
11. Another Susan alias
14. Stargirl's 9th grade friend
15. Leo had to ___ between Stargirl and his friends
16. ___ Dooks
18. First to dance with Stargirl
19. Cinnamon was one
20. MAHS basketball team fans expected to ___

Stargirl Crossword 4

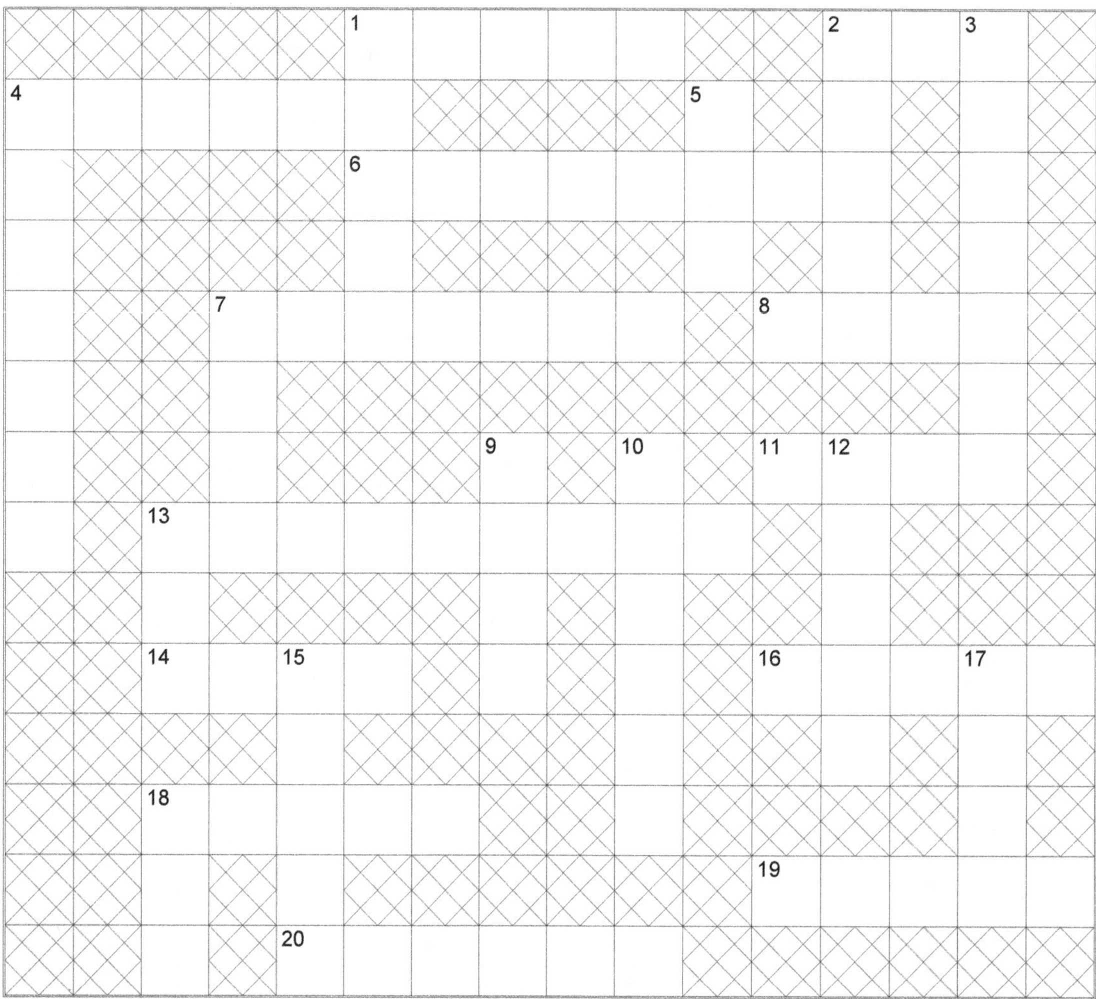

Across

1. Stargirl's bike and sidecar looked like a parade ___
2. MAHS basketball team fans expected to ___
4. Part of the newspaper Stargirl read
6. For a person so different, Stargirl's house was ___
7. Teacher who drove Susan and Leo to the state contest
8. Hot ___
11. ___ Dooks
13. The mountains
14. Danny's new one went into the trash
16. When Stargirl cries, she does not shed tears, but this
18. What Stargirl's family did after the ball
19. The Happy___held pebbles
20. Leo wanted Stargirl to do this

Down

1. The students were like mud ___ awakening
2. Hillari's boyfriend
3. Porcupine _____
4. Stargirl went to Anna's grandfather's
5. Cinnamon was one
7. ____ Area High School
9. Loyal Order of the Stone ____
10. Senor Saguaro
12. Hot Seat anchor
13. The Hot Seat jurors turned into a ___
15. Sun Valley's injured star player
17. After the state oratorical contest, Susan expected to be welcomed back like one
18. Large, extinct bird

Stargirl Crossword 4 Answer Key

					¹F	L	O	A	T		²W	I	³N	
⁴F	I	L	L	E	R				⁵R		A		E	
U					⁶O	R	D	I	N	A	R	Y	C	
N					G				T		N		K	
E			⁷M	C	S	H	A	N	E		⁸S	E	A	T
R			I										I	
A			C			⁹B		¹⁰C		¹¹U	¹²K	E	E	
¹³L	M	A	R	I	C	O	P	A	S		E			
			O			N		C			V			
	¹⁴B	¹⁵I	K	E		E		T		¹⁶L	I	G	¹⁷H	T
		O						U			N		E	
	¹⁸M	O	V	E	D			S					R	
	O		A							¹⁹W	A	G	O	N
		²⁰A	C	H	A	N	G	E						

Across
1. Stargirl's bike and sidecar looked like a parade ___
2. MAHS basketball team fans expected to ___
4. Part of the newspaper Stargirl read
6. For a person so different, Stargirl's house was ___
7. Teacher who drove Susan and Leo to the state contest
8. Hot ___
11. ___ Dooks
13. The mountains
14. Danny's new one went into the trash
16. When Stargirl cries, she does not shed tears, but this
18. What Stargirl's family did after the ball
19. The Happy___held pebbles
20. Leo wanted Stargirl to do this

Down
1. The students were like mud ___ awakening
2. Hillari's boyfriend
3. Porcupine _____
4. Stargirl went to Anna's grandfather's
5. Cinnamon was one
7. ____ Area High School
9. Loyal Order of the Stone ____
10. Senor Saguaro
12. Hot Seat anchor
13. The Hot Seat jurors turned into a ___
15. Sun Valley's injured star player
17. After the state oratorical contest, Susan expected to be welcomed back like one
18. Large, extinct bird

Stargirl

ORATORICAL	HERO	DRIVER	HEART	SENSES
FROGS	GLENDALE	CHICO	LUNCH	ROCK
PLATE	BIKE	FREE SPACE	FILLER	MUDPIE
BONE	REGAL	MOCKINGBIRD	MOVED	WIN
PLEDGE	HILLARI	MOA	DANNY	SUNFLOWER

Stargirl

NECKTIE	STARBOY	CHANGE	DORI	BASKETBALL
JURY	KOVAC	ELECTRONS	ORDINARY	BARNEY
FUNERAL	EVELYN	FREE SPACE	STARGIRL	SONORAN
MICA	UKEE	LIGHT	CHICKENS	CACTUS
BORLOCK	ENCHANTED	STALKING	RAYMOND	WAYNE

Stargirl

PLATE	GREETING	BORLOCK	MOA	SENSES
CHOOSE	WAGON	RAYMOND	FROGS	DANNY
CHANGE	CARAWAY	FREE SPACE	UKEE	BUNNY
FUNERAL	MOCKINGBIRD	LIGHT	WAYNE	CHICO
ELECTRONS	RAT	ENCHANTED	JURY	ORATORICAL

Stargirl

DORI	PARR	GLENDALE	KOVAC	BARNEY
CHEERLEADER	PETER	LUNCH	STALKING	MCSHANE
NECKTIE	STARGIRL	FREE SPACE	SEAT	TOMATO
HILLARI	EVELYN	KEVIN	ORDINARY	MARICOPAS
ARCHIE	SPINELLI	TOOLSHED	OCOTILLO	SHUNNED

BUNNY	FROGS	SPINELLI	WIN	BIKE
KEVIN	CHICO	SHUNNED	PLATE	FUNERAL
MCSHANE	SEAT	FREE SPACE	ROCK	CHANGE
ROBINEAU	STALKING	FLOAT	EVELYN	DANNY
SUNFLOWER	ARCHIE	ENCHANTED	GREETING	MOCKINGBIRD

Stargirl

PLEDGE	UKULELE	HEART	STARBOY	CHOOSE
WAGON	GLENDALE	PETER	OCOTILLO	LUNCH
MOVED	MUDPIE	FREE SPACE	MOB	MOA
MARICOPAS	BARNEY	CACTUS	NECKTIE	KOVAC
CARAWAY	TOMATO	LIGHT	SENSES	BORLOCK

Stargirl

LUNCH	EVELYN	BASKETBALL	CHEERLEADER	RAYMOND
FILLER	TOMATO	FLOAT	HEART	HERO
BUNNY	FROGS	FREE SPACE	DORI	MUDPIE
SHUNNED	ENCHANTED	REGAL	PLATE	DANNY
RAT	WIN	WAGON	MOCKINGBIRD	ROBINEAU

Stargirl

SPINELLI	ELECTRONS	MCSHANE	WAYNE	ROCK
CHICO	DRIVER	PARR	FUNERAL	ORDINARY
BIKE	NECKTIE	FREE SPACE	SEAT	HILLARI
CHOOSE	OCOTILLO	PLEDGE	MOA	MICA
STARGIRL	GREETING	BONE	KEVIN	MOB

HERO	GLENDALE	RAT	STARBOY	MCSHANE
CHEERLEADER	CHOOSE	UKEE	TOOLSHED	MOCKINGBIRD
PLATE	SUNFLOWER	FREE SPACE	MOA	CHICKENS
BONE	MICA	PETER	MOVED	RAYMOND
FROGS	WAGON	LIGHT	ORDINARY	REGAL

Stargirl

EVELYN	MARICOPAS	DRIVER	OCOTILLO	ROBINEAU
DANNY	CARAWAY	TOMATO	PLEDGE	WIN
MUDPIE	BUNNY	FREE SPACE	ENCHANTED	CACTUS
GREETING	SHUNNED	ELECTRONS	GOALPOST	SEAT
CHICO	ARCHIE	STALKING	FUNERAL	FILLER

STALKING	MOA	PARR	ORATORICAL	ROBINEAU
BORLOCK	SPINELLI	FUNERAL	BUNNY	BARNEY
MICA	ARCHIE	FREE SPACE	UKEE	TOOLSHED
PLEDGE	ELECTRONS	REGAL	OCOTILLO	CARD
SHUNNED	FLOAT	MOVED	DORI	GLENDALE

Stargirl

GOALPOST	SENSES	SONORAN	ROCK	KOVAC
CACTUS	MUDPIE	CHICKENS	RAT	PLATE
BONE	MCSHANE	FREE SPACE	SUNFLOWER	CHICO
HEART	FILLER	SEAT	BIKE	WIN
WAYNE	UKULELE	HILLARI	GREETING	ORDINARY

Stargirl

BASKETBALL	CHOOSE	RAYMOND	CHICO	FLOAT
FUNERAL	BORLOCK	MARICOPAS	HERO	PLEDGE
KEVIN	WAGON	FREE SPACE	NECKTIE	UKULELE
SUNFLOWER	CHANGE	CHEERLEADER	ORATORICAL	FILLER
BARNEY	DORI	ROBINEAU	ELECTRONS	MOCKINGBIRD

Stargirl

LUNCH	MICA	GLENDALE	ENCHANTED	REGAL
WAYNE	DANNY	BIKE	OCOTILLO	STARGIRL
BONE	CARAWAY	FREE SPACE	HEART	LIGHT
EVELYN	GOALPOST	STARBOY	CACTUS	ORDINARY
JURY	SENSES	SPINELLI	SEAT	SONORAN

Stargirl

STARGIRL	HILLARI	MOVED	HEART	ORDINARY
NECKTIE	REGAL	BIKE	MOA	FUNERAL
WIN	MOB	FREE SPACE	ENCHANTED	WAYNE
CHICKENS	SONORAN	DORI	STALKING	BORLOCK
ROCK	ROBINEAU	ORATORICAL	MARICOPAS	GLENDALE

Stargirl

MOCKINGBIRD	HERO	RAT	RAYMOND	KOVAC
EVELYN	LIGHT	WAGON	UKULELE	SENSES
UKEE	GOALPOST	FREE SPACE	BASKETBALL	OCOTILLO
BARNEY	CHOOSE	KEVIN	PETER	SEAT
SHUNNED	SPINELLI	MCSHANE	PLEDGE	SUNFLOWER

SEAT	NECKTIE	MOA	ORATORICAL	JURY
MOVED	CARAWAY	MUDPIE	ORDINARY	STALKING
WIN	PETER	FREE SPACE	BARNEY	WAGON
GOALPOST	ARCHIE	PLEDGE	ENCHANTED	MCSHANE
TOOLSHED	SPINELLI	DORI	BIKE	LIGHT

Stargirl

ROBINEAU	GREETING	MOCKINGBIRD	UKEE	FUNERAL
CARD	ELECTRONS	PARR	RAYMOND	HEART
CACTUS	FILLER	FREE SPACE	EVELYN	CHANGE
OCOTILLO	SONORAN	DRIVER	TOMATO	BUNNY
CHEERLEADER	MOB	PLATE	REGAL	HERO

Stargirl

CARD	WIN	UKULELE	HERO	GOALPOST
PLEDGE	BORLOCK	RAYMOND	ARCHIE	REGAL
ROBINEAU	WAYNE	FREE SPACE	CHICO	ENCHANTED
UKEE	HILLARI	GLENDALE	WAGON	ORDINARY
SHUNNED	ELECTRONS	LIGHT	SPINELLI	ORATORICAL

Stargirl

MOA	CACTUS	BUNNY	GREETING	CHICKENS
MOB	MOCKINGBIRD	SEAT	MUDPIE	FUNERAL
DORI	STARGIRL	FREE SPACE	EVELYN	FILLER
CHOOSE	SONORAN	DANNY	DRIVER	NECKTIE
CARAWAY	PETER	MICA	STALKING	HEART

Stargirl

KOVAC	STALKING	MICA	BONE	ENCHANTED
MOVED	CARAWAY	EVELYN	JURY	RAYMOND
FLOAT	KEVIN	FREE SPACE	WAYNE	MCSHANE
BUNNY	BASKETBALL	OCOTILLO	MOB	UKULELE
MUDPIE	ARCHIE	ORDINARY	BARNEY	FILLER

Stargirl

MARICOPAS	HERO	TOOLSHED	LIGHT	CHEERLEADER
SPINELLI	RAT	PETER	BIKE	DRIVER
CHANGE	CACTUS	FREE SPACE	UKEE	ORATORICAL
SEAT	SHUNNED	REGAL	CHOOSE	GOALPOST
WIN	CHICO	HEART	CARD	MOA

FLOAT	UKEE	MOVED	PLEDGE	CHICKENS
MCSHANE	SENSES	HEART	LUNCH	ORATORICAL
EVELYN	BASKETBALL	FREE SPACE	MARICOPAS	ELECTRONS
CACTUS	GLENDALE	DANNY	RAT	UKULELE
CHANGE	GOALPOST	BARNEY	OCOTILLO	TOMATO

Stargirl

ENCHANTED	CARAWAY	CHOOSE	MUDPIE	PLATE
ARCHIE	SHUNNED	WAYNE	STARGIRL	FILLER
RAYMOND	HERO	FREE SPACE	DRIVER	MOCKINGBIRD
BIKE	ORDINARY	KEVIN	JURY	STARBOY
ROBINEAU	SUNFLOWER	MOA	KOVAC	HILLARI

Stargirl

HEART	GOALPOST	ROBINEAU	PETER	TOMATO
PARR	DORI	STARBOY	PLATE	BONE
DANNY	BORLOCK	FREE SPACE	MCSHANE	MOCKINGBIRD
NECKTIE	STARGIRL	ORATORICAL	SPINELLI	CHOOSE
RAYMOND	GREETING	BARNEY	PLEDGE	MOVED

Stargirl

SONORAN	FILLER	REGAL	RAT	KEVIN
HILLARI	GLENDALE	SHUNNED	WAYNE	UKULELE
SEAT	CHANGE	FREE SPACE	TOOLSHED	DRIVER
CHEERLEADER	MUDPIE	BUNNY	ORDINARY	CHICO
ROCK	BASKETBALL	KOVAC	CARD	FROGS

Stargirl

CARAWAY	CHICO	MICA	MOB	PLEDGE
STALKING	SPINELLI	RAYMOND	BASKETBALL	CHOOSE
SUNFLOWER	UKULELE	FREE SPACE	SONORAN	MOVED
ROBINEAU	FLOAT	HILLARI	PETER	MOA
ORDINARY	FILLER	ENCHANTED	ELECTRONS	DRIVER

Stargirl

RAT	PLATE	DORI	FROGS	CACTUS
UKEE	MOCKINGBIRD	ORATORICAL	DANNY	TOMATO
WAGON	WAYNE	FREE SPACE	BONE	HERO
KOVAC	BUNNY	SEAT	CARD	LIGHT
EVELYN	CHICKENS	MCSHANE	GOALPOST	MARICOPAS

MOB	STARBOY	PLEDGE	BORLOCK	CHOOSE
SENSES	KEVIN	LIGHT	REGAL	DANNY
EVELYN	BARNEY	FREE SPACE	WAGON	CARAWAY
MCSHANE	BUNNY	HERO	ROCK	SPINELLI
WAYNE	PARR	ARCHIE	BIKE	KOVAC

Stargirl

UKEE	RAYMOND	FROGS	NECKTIE	SHUNNED
STARGIRL	CACTUS	ORATORICAL	PETER	CHANGE
TOMATO	UKULELE	FREE SPACE	CHEERLEADER	FUNERAL
BONE	FLOAT	GOALPOST	DORI	GLENDALE
HEART	JURY	GREETING	CHICKENS	MARICOPAS

Stargirl

MOCKINGBIRD	CARD	HERO	MUDPIE	OCOTILLO
GREETING	CHICO	TOOLSHED	CHOOSE	MOVED
BASKETBALL	PLEDGE	FREE SPACE	HILLARI	FLOAT
ROCK	MOA	WIN	DRIVER	ELECTRONS
REGAL	GOALPOST	MOB	PARR	UKULELE

Stargirl

MICA	SONORAN	ENCHANTED	WAYNE	RAT
ORATORICAL	SUNFLOWER	LUNCH	UKEE	MARICOPAS
PLATE	BORLOCK	FREE SPACE	ORDINARY	DORI
CHEERLEADER	CHICKENS	HEART	CARAWAY	MCSHANE
SENSES	BARNEY	SPINELLI	SEAT	STALKING

Stargirl Vocabulary Word List

No.	Word	Clue/Definition
1.	ABSURDITY	Something that is ridiculous or unreasonable
2.	ACQUIRED	Got
3.	ALLEGIANCE	Loyalty
4.	ANTIC	Extravagant act or gesture
5.	APPLAUD	Express approval by clapping hands
6.	APPRECIATE	To be thankful or show gratitude for
7.	ASPHALT	Pavement
8.	BAFFLE	Frustrate; puzzle
9.	BARREN	Without vegetation
10.	BIZARRE	Strikingly unconventional; odd
11.	BLITHELY	Cheerful; carefree
12.	CACTI	Plural of cactus
13.	CONCEIVED	Thought up; imagined
14.	CONFOUND	To cause to become confused
15.	CONVERGING	Approaching the same point from different directions
16.	CONVINCED	Caused to believe something
17.	CURIOUS	Eager to acquire knowledge
18.	DEVASTATION	Destruction
19.	DISPARAGED	Belittled
20.	DORMANT	Asleep; not active
21.	ELUSIVE	Can't be caught
22.	EPISODE	Incident; event
23.	FACETIOUSLY	In fun; as a joke
24.	FANATICS	People possessed by an excessive enthusiasm for something
25.	GAPED	Stared at wonderingly as with the mouth wide open
26.	HESITATE	Hold back in uncertainty
27.	HOAX	Deceitful prank
28.	IMPULSE	Urge
29.	INTERROGATE	Question
30.	ISOSCELES	Having two equal sides
31.	LINGER	Tarry; wait around
32.	LOTUS	Sitting cross-legged with the feet above the thighs
33.	MANIA	Craze; excessively popular thing to do
34.	MARQUEE	Signboard projecting over an entrance to a building
35.	MASSACRE	Slaughter
36.	MERGE	Join together
37.	MERINGUE	Fluffy pastry topping made of beaten eggs
38.	MESA	Flat-topped elevation with one or more clifflike sides
39.	MULL	Consider mentally
40.	MUNICIPAL	City
41.	NONCONFORMITY	Refusing to be bound by the accepted rules or practices of a group
42.	OBLIVIOUS	Unaware
43.	ORATORICAL	Related to public speaking
44.	PARANOID	Showing unreasonable distrust or suspicion
45.	PERPETUAL	Lasting for eternity
46.	PERSISTED	Held firmly to some purpose or undertaking despite obstacles or setbacks
47.	PRONE	Lying face down
48.	RAPTURE	Ecstasy; the state of being transported by a lofty emotion
49.	RAUCOUS	Noisy; boisterous

No.	Word	Clue/Definition
50.	REVEL	To take great pleasure or delight
51.	SERENADED	Gave a musical performance, especially one for a sweetheart
52.	SHUN	To avoid deliberately and consistently
53.	SUBDUED	Calmed; quieted
54.	SULLEN	Brooding; gloomy
55.	SWOON	Faint
56.	TENTATIVELY	Uncertainly; experimentally
57.	TRANCE	A state of detachment from one's physical surroundings
58.	UKULELE	A small four-stringed guitar
59.	UNCONVENTIONAL	Out of the ordinary; unusual
60.	VACANT	Empty
61.	VAMP	Unscrupulously seductive woman
62.	VEERED	Turned
63.	ZEAL	Enthusiasm

Stargirl Vocabulary Fill In The Blanks 1

____

____

____

____

____

____

____

____

____

____

____

____

____

____

____

____

____

____

____

____

1. To avoid deliberately and consistently

2. Showing unreasonable distrust or suspicion

3. Calmed; quieted

4. Signboard projecting over an entrance to a building

5. Unaware

6. Cheerful; carefree

7. Having two equal sides

8. Strikingly unconventional; odd

9. Fluffy pastry topping made of beaten eggs

10. Noisy; boisterous

11. Enthusiasm

12. Out of the ordinary; unusual

13. Refusing to be bound by the accepted rules or practices of a group

14. Belittled

15. Turned

16. Extravagant act or gesture

17. A state of detachment from one's physical surroundings

18. Ecstasy; the state of being transported by a lofty emotion

19. Join together

20. Express approval by clapping hands

SHUN	1. To avoid deliberately and consistently
PARANOID	2. Showing unreasonable distrust or suspicion
SUBDUED	3. Calmed; quieted
MARQUEE	4. Signboard projecting over an entrance to a building
OBLIVIOUS	5. Unaware
BLITHELY	6. Cheerful; carefree
ISOSCELES	7. Having two equal sides
BIZARRE	8. Strikingly unconventional; odd
MERINGUE	9. Fluffy pastry topping made of beaten eggs
RAUCOUS	10. Noisy; boisterous
ZEAL	11. Enthusiasm
UNCONVENTIONAL	12. Out of the ordinary; unusual
NONCONFORMITY	13. Refusing to be bound by the accepted rules or practices of a group
DISPARAGED	14. Belittled
VEERED	15. Turned
ANTIC	16. Extravagant act or gesture
TRANCE	17. A state of detachment from one's physical surroundings
RAPTURE	18. Ecstasy; the state of being transported by a lofty emotion
MERGE	19. Join together
APPLAUD	20. Express approval by clapping hands

1. Extravagant act or gesture

2. Pavement

3. Signboard projecting over an entrance to a building

4. Question

5. Incident; event

6. Gave a musical performance, especially one for a sweetheart

7. Frustrate; puzzle

8. Deceitful prank

9. Having two equal sides

10. Without vegetation

11. In fun; as a joke

12. Asleep; not active

13. A state of detachment from one's physical surroundings

14. Unscrupulously seductive woman

15. Tarry; wait around

16. Urge

17. Cheerful; carefree

18. Empty

19. Brooding; gloomy

20. Turned

ANTIC	1. Extravagant act or gesture
ASPHALT	2. Pavement
MARQUEE	3. Signboard projecting over an entrance to a building
INTERROGATE	4. Question
EPISODE	5. Incident; event
SERENADED	6. Gave a musical performance, especially one for a sweetheart
BAFFLE	7. Frustrate; puzzle
HOAX	8. Deceitful prank
ISOSCELES	9. Having two equal sides
BARREN	10. Without vegetation
FACETIOUSLY	11. In fun; as a joke
DORMANT	12. Asleep; not active
TRANCE	13. A state of detachment from one's physical surroundings
VAMP	14. Unscrupulously seductive woman
LINGER	15. Tarry; wait around
IMPULSE	16. Urge
BLITHELY	17. Cheerful; carefree
VACANT	18. Empty
SULLEN	19. Brooding; gloomy
VEERED	20. Turned

1. Plural of cactus

2. Turned

3. Caused to believe something

4. Lying face down

5. Sitting cross-legged with the feet above the thighs

6. Join together

7. Asleep; not active

8. Craze; excessively popular thing to do

9. Brooding; gloomy

10. Destruction

11. Fluffy pastry topping made of beaten eggs

12. A small four-stringed guitar

13. A state of detachment from one's physical surroundings

14. Urge

15. Cheerful; carefree

16. Without vegetation

17. Deceitful prank

18. Having two equal sides

19. Gave a musical performance, especially one for a sweetheart

20. City

CACTI	1. Plural of cactus
VEERED	2. Turned
CONVINCED	3. Caused to believe something
PRONE	4. Lying face down
LOTUS	5. Sitting cross-legged with the feet above the thighs
MERGE	6. Join together
DORMANT	7. Asleep; not active
MANIA	8. Craze; excessively popular thing to do
SULLEN	9. Brooding; gloomy
DEVASTATION	10. Destruction
MERINGUE	11. Fluffy pastry topping made of beaten eggs
UKULELE	12. A small four-stringed guitar
TRANCE	13. A state of detachment from one's physical surroundings
IMPULSE	14. Urge
BLITHELY	15. Cheerful; carefree
BARREN	16. Without vegetation
HOAX	17. Deceitful prank
ISOSCELES	18. Having two equal sides
SERENADED	19. Gave a musical performance, especially one for a sweetheart
MUNICIPAL	20. City

1. Faint

2. Signboard projecting over an entrance to a building

3. Deceitful prank

4. Unscrupulously seductive woman

5. Express approval by clapping hands

6. Consider mentally

7. Brooding; gloomy

8. Unaware

9. Having two equal sides

10. Held firmly to some purpose or undertaking despite obstacles or setbacks
11. To avoid deliberately and consistently

12. Incident; event

13. Gave a musical performance, especially one for a sweetheart
14. Eager to acquire knowledge

15. City

16. Loyalty

17. Join together

18. Cheerful; carefree

19. Lasting for eternity

20. Thought up; imagined

SWOON	1. Faint
MARQUEE	2. Signboard projecting over an entrance to a building
HOAX	3. Deceitful prank
VAMP	4. Unscrupulously seductive woman
APPLAUD	5. Express approval by clapping hands
MULL	6. Consider mentally
SULLEN	7. Brooding; gloomy
OBLIVIOUS	8. Unaware
ISOSCELES	9. Having two equal sides
PERSISTED	10. Held firmly to some purpose or undertaking despite obstacles or setbacks
SHUN	11. To avoid deliberately and consistently
EPISODE	12. Incident; event
SERENADED	13. Gave a musical performance, especially one for a sweetheart
CURIOUS	14. Eager to acquire knowledge
MUNICIPAL	15. City
ALLEGIANCE	16. Loyalty
MERGE	17. Join together
BLITHELY	18. Cheerful; carefree
PERPETUAL	19. Lasting for eternity
CONCEIVED	20. Thought up; imagined

Stargirl Vocabulary Matching 1

___ 1. EPISODE   A. Noisy; boisterous

___ 2. MERINGUE   B. Cheerful; carefree

___ 3. MULL   C. Craze; excessively popular thing to do

___ 4. ASPHALT   D. Thought up; imagined

___ 5. VAMP   E. To be thankful or show gratitude for

___ 6. NONCONFORMITY   F. Approaching the same point from different directions

___ 7. CONVINCED   G. Urge

___ 8. MARQUEE   H. Held firmly to some purpose or undertaking despite
                                     obstacles or setbacks

___ 9. CONVERGING   I. Belittled

___10. PARANOID   J. Incident; event

___11. GAPED   K. Signboard projecting over an entrance to a building

___12. CACTI   L. Consider mentally

___13. CONCEIVED   M. Refusing to be bound by the accepted rules or
                                     practices of a group

___14. SUBDUED   N. Plural of cactus

___15. MANIA   O. Pavement

___16. PERSISTED   P. Showing unreasonable distrust or suspicion

___17. UNCONVENTIONAL   Q. Related to public speaking

___18. ANTIC   R. Caused to believe something

___19. ZEAL   S. Enthusiasm

___20. DISPARAGED   T. Out of the ordinary; unusual

___21. IMPULSE   U. Stared at wonderingly as with the mouth wide open

___22. BLITHELY   V. Extravagant act or gesture

___23. APPRECIATE   W. Calmed; quieted

___24. RAUCOUS   X. Unscrupulously seductive woman

___25. ORATORICAL   Y. Fluffy pastry topping made of beaten eggs

J - 1. EPISODE	A. Noisy; boisterous
Y - 2. MERINGUE	B. Cheerful; carefree
L - 3. MULL	C. Craze; excessively popular thing to do
O - 4. ASPHALT	D. Thought up; imagined
X - 5. VAMP	E. To be thankful or show gratitude for
M - 6. NONCONFORMITY	F. Approaching the same point from different directions
R - 7. CONVINCED	G. Urge
K - 8. MARQUEE	H. Held firmly to some purpose or undertaking despite obstacles or setbacks
F - 9. CONVERGING	I. Belittled
P -10. PARANOID	J. Incident; event
U -11. GAPED	K. Signboard projecting over an entrance to a building
N -12. CACTI	L. Consider mentally
D -13. CONCEIVED	M. Refusing to be bound by the accepted rules or practices of a group
W -14. SUBDUED	N. Plural of cactus
C -15. MANIA	O. Pavement
H -16. PERSISTED	P. Showing unreasonable distrust or suspicion
T -17. UNCONVENTIONAL	Q. Related to public speaking
V -18. ANTIC	R. Caused to believe something
S -19. ZEAL	S. Enthusiasm
I - 20. DISPARAGED	T. Out of the ordinary; unusual
G -21. IMPULSE	U. Stared at wonderingly as with the mouth wide open
B -22. BLITHELY	V. Extravagant act or gesture
E -23. APPRECIATE	W. Calmed; quieted
A -24. RAUCOUS	X. Unscrupulously seductive woman
Q -25. ORATORICAL	Y. Fluffy pastry topping made of beaten eggs

Stargirl Vocabulary Matching 2

___ 1. LOTUS	A. Unaware
___ 2. CONVINCED	B. Caused to believe something
___ 3. MARQUEE	C. Sitting cross-legged with the feet above the thighs
___ 4. FACETIOUSLY	D. Extravagant act or gesture
___ 5. INTERROGATE	E. Frustrate; puzzle
___ 6. BAFFLE	F. Something that is ridiculous or unreasonable
___ 7. ABSURDITY	G. Got
___ 8. CURIOUS	H. Gave a musical performance, especially one for a sweetheart
___ 9. ACQUIRED	I. Showing unreasonable distrust or suspicion
___10. OBLIVIOUS	J. Flat-topped elevation with one or more clifflike sides
___11. VAMP	K. Can't be caught
___12. REVEL	L. Join together
___13. MULL	M. Without vegetation
___14. BIZARRE	N. Strikingly unconventional; odd
___15. UNCONVENTIONAL	O. Out of the ordinary; unusual
___16. SERENADED	P. In fun; as a joke
___17. DISPARAGED	Q. Signboard projecting over an entrance to a building
___18. PARANOID	R. Loyalty
___19. MERGE	S. To take great pleasure or delight
___20. MESA	T. Unscrupulously seductive woman
___21. ALLEGIANCE	U. Belittled
___22. ELUSIVE	V. Question
___23. ANTIC	W. Consider mentally
___24. DORMANT	X. Asleep; not active
___25. BARREN	Y. Eager to acquire knowledge

Stargirl Vocabulary Matching 2 Answer Key

C - 1. LOTUS

B - 2. CONVINCED

Q - 3. MARQUEE

P - 4. FACETIOUSLY

V - 5. INTERROGATE

E - 6. BAFFLE

F - 7. ABSURDITY

Y - 8. CURIOUS

G - 9. ACQUIRED

A -10. OBLIVIOUS

T -11. VAMP

S -12. REVEL

W -13. MULL

N -14. BIZARRE

O -15. UNCONVENTIONAL

H -16. SERENADED

U -17. DISPARAGED

I - 18. PARANOID

L - 19. MERGE

J - 20. MESA

R -21. ALLEGIANCE

K -22. ELUSIVE

D -23. ANTIC

X -24. DORMANT

M -25. BARREN

A. Unaware

B. Caused to believe something

C. Sitting cross-legged with the feet above the thighs

D. Extravagant act or gesture

E. Frustrate; puzzle

F. Something that is ridiculous or unreasonable

G. Got

H. Gave a musical performance, especially one for a sweetheart

I. Showing unreasonable distrust or suspicion

J. Flat-topped elevation with one or more clifflike sides

K. Can't be caught

L. Join together

M. Without vegetation

N. Strikingly unconventional; odd

O. Out of the ordinary; unusual

P. In fun; as a joke

Q. Signboard projecting over an entrance to a building

R. Loyalty

S. To take great pleasure or delight

T. Unscrupulously seductive woman

U. Belittled

V. Question

W. Consider mentally

X. Asleep; not active

Y. Eager to acquire knowledge

___ 1. BIZARRE	A.	Signboard projecting over an entrance to a building
___ 2. FACETIOUSLY	B.	A state of detachment from one's physical surroundings
___ 3. MASSACRE	C.	Loyalty
___ 4. DEVASTATION	D.	Showing unreasonable distrust or suspicion
___ 5. SULLEN	E.	Empty
___ 6. PARANOID	F.	In fun; as a joke
___ 7. ALLEGIANCE	G.	Destruction
___ 8. RAUCOUS	H.	Caused to believe something
___ 9. TRANCE	I.	Tarry; wait around
___10. CURIOUS	J.	Noisy; boisterous
___11. FANATICS	K.	Cheerful; carefree
___12. NONCONFORMITY	L.	Extravagant act or gesture
___13. CACTI	M.	Strikingly unconventional; odd
___14. VAMP	N.	Slaughter
___15. CONVINCED	O.	Flat-topped elevation with one or more clifflike sides
___16. LINGER	P.	Belittled
___17. PERSISTED	Q.	People possessed by an excessive enthusiasm for something
___18. DISPARAGED	R.	Approaching the same point from different directions
___19. MESA	S.	Fluffy pastry topping made of beaten eggs
___20. MARQUEE	T.	Brooding; gloomy
___21. BLITHELY	U.	Held firmly to some purpose or undertaking despite obstacles or setbacks
___22. ANTIC	V.	Plural of cactus
___23. VACANT	W.	Refusing to be bound by the accepted rules or practices of a group
___24. CONVERGING	X.	Eager to acquire knowledge
___25. MERINGUE	Y.	Unscrupulously seductive woman

M - 1. BIZARRE

F - 2. FACETIOUSLY

N - 3. MASSACRE

G - 4. DEVASTATION

T - 5. SULLEN

D - 6. PARANOID

C - 7. ALLEGIANCE

J - 8. RAUCOUS

B - 9. TRANCE

X - 10. CURIOUS

Q - 11. FANATICS

W - 12. NONCONFORMITY

V - 13. CACTI

Y - 14. VAMP

H - 15. CONVINCED

I - 16. LINGER

U - 17. PERSISTED

P - 18. DISPARAGED

O - 19. MESA

A - 20. MARQUEE

K - 21. BLITHELY

L - 22. ANTIC

E - 23. VACANT

R - 24. CONVERGING

S - 25. MERINGUE

A. Signboard projecting over an entrance to a building

B. A state of detachment from one's physical surroundings

C. Loyalty

D. Showing unreasonable distrust or suspicion

E. Empty

F. In fun; as a joke

G. Destruction

H. Caused to believe something

I. Tarry; wait around

J. Noisy; boisterous

K. Cheerful; carefree

L. Extravagant act or gesture

M. Strikingly unconventional; odd

N. Slaughter

O. Flat-topped elevation with one or more clifflike sides

P. Belittled

Q. People possessed by an excessive enthusiasm for something

R. Approaching the same point from different directions

S. Fluffy pastry topping made of beaten eggs

T. Brooding; gloomy

U. Held firmly to some purpose or undertaking despite obstacles or setbacks

V. Plural of cactus

W. Refusing to be bound by the accepted rules or practices of a group

X. Eager to acquire knowledge

Y. Unscrupulously seductive woman

Stargirl Vocabulary Matching 4

___ 1. SULLEN	A. Empty
___ 2. ZEAL	B. Flat-topped elevation with one or more clifflike sides
___ 3. ASPHALT	C. Plural of cactus
___ 4. REVEL	D. Unscrupulously seductive woman
___ 5. SUBDUED	E. Question
___ 6. PERPETUAL	F. Consider mentally
___ 7. PARANOID	G. Lasting for eternity
___ 8. VACANT	H. Showing unreasonable distrust or suspicion
___ 9. MESA	I. In fun; as a joke
___10. DORMANT	J. Unaware
___11. GAPED	K. To take great pleasure or delight
___12. OBLIVIOUS	L. Brooding; gloomy
___13. FACETIOUSLY	M. Signboard projecting over an entrance to a building
___14. VAMP	N. Enthusiasm
___15. MANIA	O. Fluffy pastry topping made of beaten eggs
___16. ELUSIVE	P. Can't be caught
___17. MERGE	Q. Calmed; quieted
___18. APPLAUD	R. Craze; excessively popular thing to do
___19. MERINGUE	S. Join together
___20. MULL	T. Got
___21. CACTI	U. Without vegetation
___22. ACQUIRED	V. Asleep; not active
___23. MARQUEE	W. Pavement
___24. BARREN	X. Stared at wonderingly as with the mouth wide open
___25. INTERROGATE	Y. Express approval by clapping hands

Stargirl Vocabulary Matching 4 Answer Key

L - 1. SULLEN   A. Empty

N - 2. ZEAL   B. Flat-topped elevation with one or more clifflike sides

W - 3. ASPHALT   C. Plural of cactus

K - 4. REVEL   D. Unscrupulously seductive woman

Q - 5. SUBDUED   E. Question

G - 6. PERPETUAL   F. Consider mentally

H - 7. PARANOID   G. Lasting for eternity

A - 8. VACANT   H. Showing unreasonable distrust or suspicion

B - 9. MESA   I. In fun; as a joke

V -10. DORMANT   J. Unaware

X -11. GAPED   K. To take great pleasure or delight

J - 12. OBLIVIOUS   L. Brooding; gloomy

I - 13. FACETIOUSLY   M. Signboard projecting over an entrance to a building

D -14. VAMP   N. Enthusiasm

R -15. MANIA   O. Fluffy pastry topping made of beaten eggs

P -16. ELUSIVE   P. Can't be caught

S -17. MERGE   Q. Calmed; quieted

Y -18. APPLAUD   R. Craze; excessively popular thing to do

O -19. MERINGUE   S. Join together

F -20. MULL   T. Got

C -21. CACTI   U. Without vegetation

T -22. ACQUIRED   V. Asleep; not active

M -23. MARQUEE   W. Pavement

U -24. BARREN   X. Stared at wonderingly as with the mouth wide open

E -25. INTERROGATE   Y. Express approval by clapping hands

Stargirl Vocabulary Magic Squares 1

Match the definition with the vocabulary word. Put your answers in the magic squares below. When your answers are correct, all columns and rows will add to the same number.

A. BIZARRE
B. DORMANT
C. RAUCOUS
D. SULLEN
E. ELUSIVE
F. CURIOUS

G. PERPETUAL
H. VACANT
I. EPISODE
J. CONCEIVED
K. ISOSCELES
L. LOTUS

M. INTERROGATE
N. HESITATE
O. CONVERGING
P. REVEL

1. Empty
2. Strikingly unconventional; odd
3. Asleep; not active
4. Lasting for eternity
5. Thought up; imagined
6. Approaching the same point from different directions
7. To take great pleasure or delight
8. Incident; event
9. Having two equal sides
10. Hold back in uncertainty
11. Question
12. Sitting cross-legged with the feet above the thighs
13. Can't be caught
14. Brooding; gloomy
15. Noisy; boisterous
16. Eager to acquire knowledge

A=	B=	C=	D=
E=	F=	G=	H=
I=	J=	K=	L=
M=	N=	O=	P=

Stargirl Vocabulary Magic Squares 1 Answer Key

Match the definition with the vocabulary word. Put your answers in the magic squares below. When your answers are correct, all columns and rows will add to the same number.

A. BIZARRE
B. DORMANT
C. RAUCOUS
D. SULLEN
E. ELUSIVE
F. CURIOUS

G. PERPETUAL
H. VACANT
I. EPISODE
J. CONCEIVED
K. ISOSCELES
L. LOTUS

M. INTERROGATE
N. HESITATE
O. CONVERGING
P. REVEL

1. Empty
2. Strikingly unconventional; odd
3. Asleep; not active
4. Lasting for eternity
5. Thought up; imagined
6. Approaching the same point from different directions
7. To take great pleasure or delight
8. Incident; event
9. Having two equal sides
10. Hold back in uncertainty
11. Question
12. Sitting cross-legged with the feet above the thighs
13. Can't be caught
14. Brooding; gloomy
15. Noisy; boisterous
16. Eager to acquire knowledge

A=2	B=3	C=15	D=14
E=13	F=16	G=4	H=1
I=8	J=5	K=9	L=12
M=11	N=10	O=6	P=7

Stargirl Vocabulary Magic Squares 2

Match the definition with the vocabulary word. Put your answers in the magic squares below. When your answers are correct, all columns and rows will add to the same number.

A. MERINGUE
B. BAFFLE
C. CONCEIVED
D. MUNICIPAL
E. MASSACRE
F. IMPULSE

G. APPLAUD
H. DISPARAGED
I. TENTATIVELY
J. SHUN
K. RAUCOUS
L. SWOON

M. SUBDUED
N. ISOSCELES
O. GAPED
P. MERGE

1. Fluffy pastry topping made of beaten eggs
2. Having two equal sides
3. To avoid deliberately and consistently
4. Slaughter
5. Express approval by clapping hands
6. Faint
7. Join together
8. Thought up; imagined
9. Stared at wonderingly as with the mouth wide open
10. City
11. Belittled
12. Noisy; boisterous
13. Uncertainly; experimentally
14. Urge
15. Frustrate; puzzle
16. Calmed; quieted

A=	B=	C=	D=
E=	F=	G=	H=
I=	J=	K=	L=
M=	N=	O=	P=

Stargirl Vocabulary Magic Squares 2 Answer Key

Match the definition with the vocabulary word. Put your answers in the magic squares below. When your answers are correct, all columns and rows will add to the same number.

A. MERINGUE	G. APPLAUD	M. SUBDUED
B. BAFFLE	H. DISPARAGED	N. ISOSCELES
C. CONCEIVED	I. TENTATIVELY	O. GAPED
D. MUNICIPAL	J. SHUN	P. MERGE
E. MASSACRE	K. RAUCOUS	
F. IMPULSE	L. SWOON	

1. Fluffy pastry topping made of beaten eggs
2. Having two equal sides
3. To avoid deliberately and consistently
4. Slaughter
5. Express approval by clapping hands
6. Faint
7. Join together
8. Thought up; imagined
9. Stared at wonderingly as with the mouth wide open
10. City
11. Belittled
12. Noisy; boisterous
13. Uncertainly; experimentally
14. Urge
15. Frustrate; puzzle
16. Calmed; quieted

A=1	B=15	C=8	D=10
E=4	F=14	G=5	H=11
I=13	J=3	K=12	L=6
M=16	N=2	O=9	P=7

Stargirl Vocabulary Magic Squares 3

Match the definition with the vocabulary word. Put your answers in the magic squares below. When your answers are correct, all columns and rows will add to the same number.

A. OBLIVIOUS

B. MARQUEE

C. MERINGUE

D. FACETIOUSLY

E. INTERROGATE

F. IMPULSE

G. GAPED

H. HESITATE

I. REVEL

J. ALLEGIANCE

K. ACQUIRED

L. SWOON

M. ZEAL

N. VEERED

O. VACANT

P. FANATICS

1. Hold back in uncertainty
2. Enthusiasm
3. Signboard projecting over an entrance to a building
4. Got
5. Loyalty
6. Fluffy pastry topping made of beaten eggs
7. People possessed by an excessive enthusiasm for something
8. Question

9. Empty
10. Urge
11. To take great pleasure or delight
12. In fun; as a joke
13. Unaware
14. Faint
15. Stared at wonderingly as with the mouth wide open
16. Turned

A=	B=	C=	D=
E=	F=	G=	H=
I=	J=	K=	L=
M=	N=	O=	P=

Stargirl Vocabulary Magic Squares 3 Answer Key

Match the definition with the vocabulary word. Put your answers in the magic squares below. When your answers are correct, all columns and rows will add to the same number.

A. OBLIVIOUS
B. MARQUEE
C. MERINGUE
D. FACETIOUSLY
E. INTERROGATE
F. IMPULSE

G. GAPED
H. HESITATE
I. REVEL
J. ALLEGIANCE
K. ACQUIRED
L. SWOON

M. ZEAL
N. VEERED
O. VACANT
P. FANATICS

1. Hold back in uncertainty
2. Enthusiasm
3. Signboard projecting over an entrance to a building
4. Got
5. Loyalty
6. Fluffy pastry topping made of beaten eggs
7. People possessed by an excessive enthusiasm for something
8. Question
9. Empty
10. Urge
11. To take great pleasure or delight
12. In fun; as a joke
13. Unaware
14. Faint
15. Stared at wonderingly as with the mouth wide open
16. Turned

A=13	B=3	C=6	D=12
E=8	F=10	G=15	H=1
I=11	J=5	K=4	L=14
M=2	N=16	O=9	P=7

Stargirl Vocabulary Magic Squares 4

Match the definition with the vocabulary word. Put your answers in the magic squares below. When your answers are correct, all columns and rows will add to the same number.

A. DORMANT
B. BARREN
C. SWOON
D. MARQUEE
E. CONFOUND
F. ASPHALT

G. CONVERGING
H. DEVASTATION
I. CONCEIVED
J. PARANOID
K. MULL
L. SERENADED

M. UNCONVENTIONAL
N. HOAX
O. BIZARRE
P. FANATICS

1. Faint
2. Showing unreasonable distrust or suspicion
3. Pavement
4. Strikingly unconventional; odd
5. People possessed by an excessive enthusiasm for something
6. To cause to become confused
7. Thought up; imagined
8. Signboard projecting over an entrance to a building
9. Out of the ordinary; unusual
10. Destruction
11. Gave a musical performance, especially one for a sweetheart
12. Asleep; not active
13. Without vegetation
14. Consider mentally
15. Approaching the same point from different directions
16. Deceitful prank

A=	B=	C=	D=
E=	F=	G=	H=
I=	J=	K=	L=
M=	N=	O=	P=

Stargirl Vocabulary Magic Squares 4 Answer Key

Match the definition with the vocabulary word. Put your answers in the magic squares below. When your answers are correct, all columns and rows will add to the same number.

A. DORMANT
B. BARREN
C. SWOON
D. MARQUEE
E. CONFOUND
F. ASPHALT

G. CONVERGING
H. DEVASTATION
I. CONCEIVED
J. PARANOID
K. MULL
L. SERENADED

M. UNCONVENTIONAL
N. HOAX
O. BIZARRE
P. FANATICS

1. Faint
2. Showing unreasonable distrust or suspicion
3. Pavement
4. Strikingly unconventional; odd
5. People possessed by an excessive enthusiasm for something
6. To cause to become confused
7. Thought up; imagined
8. Signboard projecting over an entrance to a building

9. Out of the ordinary; unusual
10. Destruction
11. Gave a musical performance, especially one for a sweetheart
12. Asleep; not active
13. Without vegetation
14. Consider mentally
15. Approaching the same point from different directions
16. Deceitful prank

A=12	B=13	C=1	D=8
E=6	F=3	G=15	H=10
I=7	J=2	K=14	L=11
M=9	N=16	O=4	P=5

Stargirl Vocabulary Word Search 1

Words are placed backwards, forward, diagonally, up and down. Clues listed below can help you find the words. Circle the hidden vocabulary words in the maze.

```
D  E  V  A  S  T  A  T  I  O  N  E  L  U  S  I  V  E  H
N  D  S  L  P  P  K  D  D  B  V  L  E  M  W  W  R  W  H
G  V  W  I  H  M  C  A  K  L  A  S  V  E  O  M  A  R  W
V  A  G  N  Z  V  U  P  N  O  L  R  E  R  O  U  P  H  B
H  N  P  G  E  I  R  P  H  T  H  P  R  G  N  L  T  E  B
D  Y  L  E  H  T  I  L  B  U  I  Y  N  E  L  L  U  S  K
N  I  R  R  D  C  O  A  V  S  L  C  S  H  N  G  R  I  Z
S  E  S  R  N  A  U  U  O  S  J  L  Z  Z  N  G  E  T  C
D  M  D  P  S  C  S  D  U  W  U  E  C  I  C  X  X  A  J
E  E  I  T  A  M  E  O  P  P  A  L  R  W  A  H  M  T  H
T  S  O  G  W  R  I  M  M  L  N  E  N  O  C  R  A  E  S
S  A  N  C  Z  T  A  I  A  M  M  L  H  S  H  U  N  R  Z
I  S  A  M  E  N  F  G  N  R  P  U  P  P  B  C  I  R  V
S  F  R  C  C  A  Q  F  E  L  Q  K  Y  R  A  W  A  A  R
R  Q  A  K  N  C  D  E  U  D  B  U  S  O  F  P  M  Z  G
E  F  P  F  A  A  S  P  H  A  L  T  E  N  F  P  L  I  G
P  M  C  H  R  V  W  T  I  S  O  S  C  E  L  E  S  B  W
F  A  N  A  T  I  C  S  Y  G  N  I  G  R  E  V  N  O  C
```

A small four-stringed guitar (7)
A state of detachment from one's physical surroundings (6)
Approaching the same point from different directions (10)
Belittled (10)
Brooding; gloomy (6)
Calmed; quieted (7)
Can't be caught (7)
Cheerful; carefree (8)
Consider mentally (4)
Craze; excessively popular thing to do (5)
Deceitful prank (4)
Destruction (11)
Eager to acquire knowledge (7)
Ecstasy; the state of being transported by a lofty emotion (7)
Empty (6)
Enthusiasm (4)
Express approval by clapping hands (7)
Extravagant act or gesture (5)
Faint (5)
Flat-topped elevation with one or more clifflike sides (4)
Fluffy pastry topping made of beaten eggs (8)
Frustrate; puzzle (6)
Having two equal sides (9)

Held firmly to some purpose or undertaking despite obstacles or setbacks (9)
Hold back in uncertainty (8)
In fun; as a joke (11)
Incident; event (7)
Join together (5)
Lying face down (5)
Pavement (7)
People possessed by an excessive enthusiasm for something (8)
Plural of cactus (5)
Showing unreasonable distrust or suspicion (8)
Signboard projecting over an entrance to a building (7)
Sitting cross-legged with the feet above the thighs (5)
Stared at wonderingly as with the mouth wide open (5)
Strikingly unconventional; odd (7)
Tarry; wait around (6)
To avoid deliberately and consistently (4)
To take great pleasure or delight (5)
Turned (6)
Unscrupulously seductive woman (4)
Urge (7)
Without vegetation (6)

Words are placed backwards, forward, diagonally, up and down. Clues listed below can help you find the words. Circle the hidden vocabulary words in the maze.

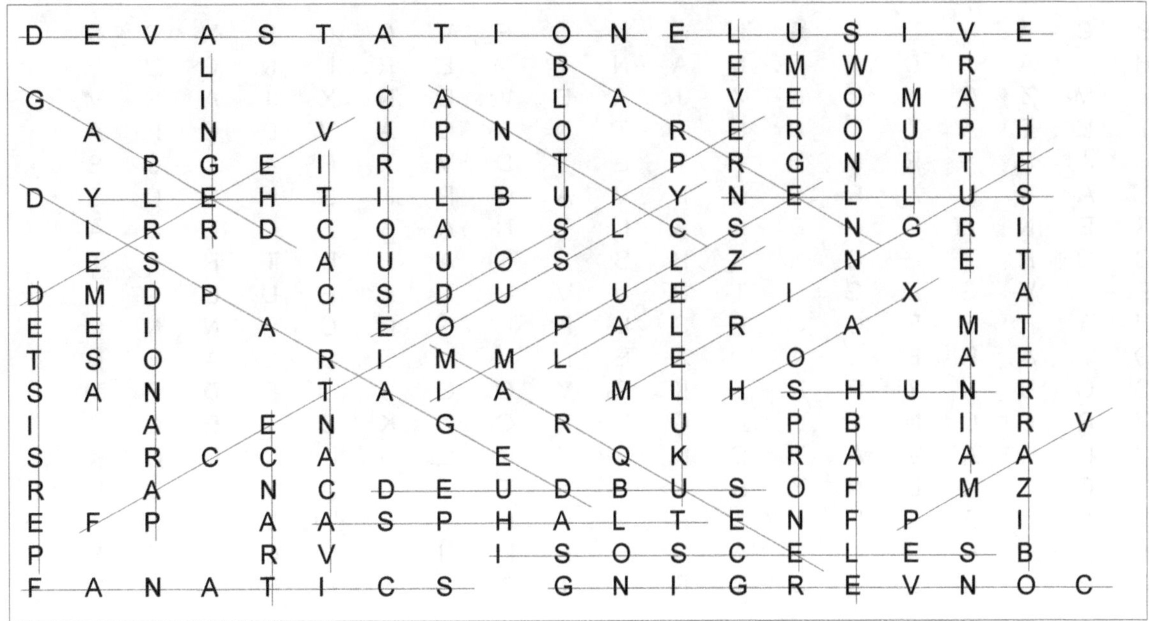

A small four-stringed guitar (7)

A state of detachment from one's physical surroundings (6)

Approaching the same point from different directions (10)

Belittled (10)

Brooding; gloomy (6)

Calmed; quieted (7)

Can't be caught (7)

Cheerful; carefree (8)

Consider mentally (4)

Craze; excessively popular thing to do (5)

Deceitful prank (4)

Destruction (11)

Eager to acquire knowledge (7)

Ecstasy; the state of being transported by a lofty emotion (7)

Empty (6)

Enthusiasm (4)

Express approval by clapping hands (7)

Extravagant act or gesture (5)

Faint (5)

Flat-topped elevation with one or more clifflike sides (4)

Fluffy pastry topping made of beaten eggs (8)

Frustrate; puzzle (6)

Having two equal sides (9)

Held firmly to some purpose or undertaking despite obstacles or setbacks (9)

Hold back in uncertainty (8)

In fun; as a joke (11)

Incident; event (7)

Join together (5)

Lying face down (5)

Pavement (7)

People possessed by an excessive enthusiasm for something (8)

Plural of cactus (5)

Showing unreasonable distrust or suspicion (8)

Signboard projecting over an entrance to a building (7)

Sitting cross-legged with the feet above the thighs (5)

Stared at wonderingly as with the mouth wide open (5)

Strikingly unconventional; odd (7)

Tarry; wait around (6)

To avoid deliberately and consistently (4)

To take great pleasure or delight (5)

Turned (6)

Unscrupulously seductive woman (4)

Urge (7)

Without vegetation (6)

Stargirl Vocabulary Word Search 2

Words are placed backwards, forward, diagonally, up and down. Clues listed below can help you find the words. Circle the hidden vocabulary words in the maze.

```
B  C  A  L  L  E  G  I  A  N  C  E  V  C  D  R  N  C  D
H  I  A  J  D  O  R  M  A  N  T  M  E  R  I  N  G  U  E
Y  M  Z  C  H  X  N  Z  J  A  E  W  D  N  X  J  A  R  V
T  E  E  A  T  T  U  L  T  T  N  A  C  A  V  L  C  I  A
I  J  P  S  R  I  H  I  T  E  T  D  V  X  P  A  Y  O  S
M  A  N  I  A  R  S  D  L  V  A  M  P  P  S  L  S  U  T
R  E  N  W  S  E  E  I  A  I  T  N  A  S  E  O  E  S  A
O  O  R  T  H  O  N  K  H  S  I  S  A  H  L  T  R  C  T
F  R  V  G  I  G  D  T  P  U  V  M  T  L  E  U  E  O  I
N  A  R  E  E  C  G  E  S  L  E  I  G  D  C  S  N  N  O
O  T  A  R  E  L  A  N  A  E  L  V  I  Z  S  G  A  F  N
C  O  U  H  Y  R  P  Z  K  B  Y  O  Q  U  O  R  D  O  M
N  R  C  O  N  V  E  R  G  I  N  G  E  K  S  T  E  U  F
O  I  O  A  V  A  D  D  N  A  N  C  L  U  I  W  D  N  K
N  C  U  X  L  N  Y  B  R  V  N  E  L  L  B  V  O  D  D
Y  A  S  E  L  F  F  A  B  A  V  L  T  E  W  M  Q  O  Z
K  L  E  R  U  T  P  A  R  E  E  M  U  L  L  C  C  Q  N
P  R  O  N  E  K  M  T  R  N  J  Z  N  E  R  R  A  B  H
```

A small four-stringed guitar (7)
A state of detachment from one's physical surroundings (6)
Approaching the same point from different directions (10)
Asleep; not active (7)
Brooding; gloomy (6)
Can't be caught (7)
Cheerful; carefree (8)
Consider mentally (4)
Craze; excessively popular thing to do (5)
Deceitful prank (4)
Destruction (11)
Eager to acquire knowledge (7)
Ecstasy; the state of being transported by a lofty emotion (7)
Empty (6)
Enthusiasm (4)
Express approval by clapping hands (7)
Extravagant act or gesture (5)
Faint (5)
Flat-topped elevation with one or more clifflike sides (4)
Fluffy pastry topping made of beaten eggs (8)
Frustrate; puzzle (6)
Gave a musical performance, especially one for a sweetheart (9)

Having two equal sides (9)
Hold back in uncertainty (8)
Incident; event (7)
Join together (5)
Loyalty (10)
Lying face down (5)
Noisy; boisterous (7)
Pavement (7)
Plural of cactus (5)
Refusing to be bound by the accepted rules or practices of a group (13)
Related to public speaking (10)
Showing unreasonable distrust or suspicion (8)
Sitting cross-legged with the feet above the thighs (5)
Slaughter (8)
Stared at wonderingly as with the mouth wide open (5)
Strikingly unconventional; odd (7)
Tarry; wait around (6)
To cause to become confused (8)
To avoid deliberately and consistently (4)
To take great pleasure or delight (5)
Turned (6)
Uncertainly; experimentally (11)
Unscrupulously seductive woman (4)
Without vegetation (6)

Stargirl Vocabulary Word Search 2 Answer Key

Words are placed backwards, forward, diagonally, up and down. Clues listed below can help you find the words. Circle the hidden vocabulary words in the maze.

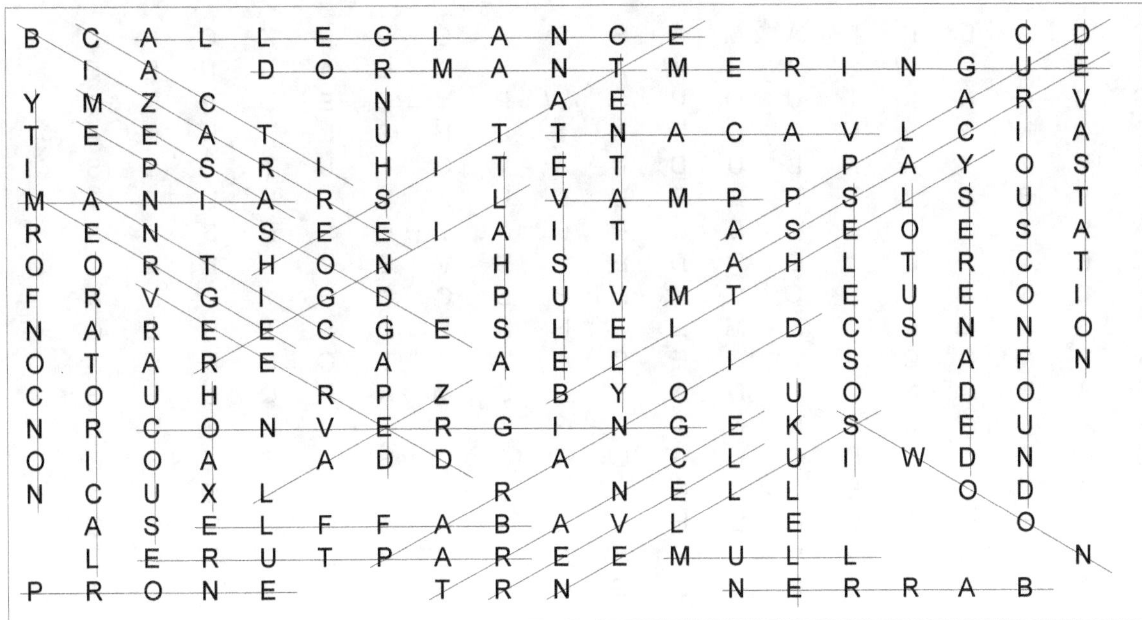

A small four-stringed guitar (7)

A state of detachment from one's physical surroundings (6)

Approaching the same point from different directions (10)

Asleep; not active (7)

Brooding; gloomy (6)

Can't be caught (7)

Cheerful; carefree (8)

Consider mentally (4)

Craze; excessively popular thing to do (5)

Deceitful prank (4)

Destruction (11)

Eager to acquire knowledge (7)

Ecstasy; the state of being transported by a lofty emotion (7)

Empty (6)

Enthusiasm (4)

Express approval by clapping hands (7)

Extravagant act or gesture (5)

Faint (5)

Flat-topped elevation with one or more clifflike sides (4)

Fluffy pastry topping made of beaten eggs (8)

Frustrate; puzzle (6)

Gave a musical performance, especially one for a sweetheart (9)

Having two equal sides (9)

Hold back in uncertainty (8)

Incident; event (7)

Join together (5)

Loyalty (10)

Lying face down (5)

Noisy; boisterous (7)

Pavement (7)

Plural of cactus (5)

Refusing to be bound by the accepted rules or practices of a group (13)

Related to public speaking (10)

Showing unreasonable distrust or suspicion (8)

Sitting cross-legged with the feet above the thighs (5)

Slaughter (8)

Stared at wonderingly as with the mouth wide open (5)

Strikingly unconventional; odd (7)

Tarry; wait around (6)

To cause to become confused (8)

To avoid deliberately and consistently (4)

To take great pleasure or delight (5)

Turned (6)

Uncertainly; experimentally (11)

Unscrupulously seductive woman (4)

Without vegetation (6)

Stargirl Vocabulary Word Search 3

Words are placed backwards, forward, diagonally, up and down. Words listed below are included in the maze. Circle the hidden vocabulary words in the maze.

D	U	A	L	P	P	A	M	A	S	S	A	C	R	E	X	C	P	D
I	A	Z	U	W	S	Y	S	W	X	E	H	A	Q	A	B	U	E	E
S	C	O	N	K	T	U	O	P	S	W	P	Y	O	E	L	R	R	V
P	Q	K	R	P	U	O	B	L	H	T	D	H	S	L	I	I	P	A
A	U	W	Y	A	N	L	U	D	U	A	Y	Q	L	U	T	O	E	S
R	I	B	L	V	T	P	E	R	U	L	L	Z	Y	S	H	U	T	T
A	R	J	C	D	M	O	E	L	P	E	A	T	H	I	E	S	U	A
G	E	T	S	I	J	C	R	D	E	L	D	V	E	V	L	R	A	T
E	D	N	M	F	N	O	L	I	L	F	D	C	S	E	Y	I	L	I
D	H	A	M	E	C	N	M	E	C	F	N	Y	I	S	T	P	S	O
J	P	M	R	C	R	V	G	E	C	A	W	R	T	C	M	N	S	N
P	A	R	A	N	O	I	D	A	R	B	L	M	A	R	Q	U	E	E
T	A	O	O	C	A	N	N	T	P	G	K	C	T	U	L	W	L	Q
B	M	D	I	N	D	C	F	G	L	E	E	W	E	L	C	Y	S	L
B	A	T	C	V	E	E	S	O	U	O	D	V	E	V	G	O	E	Q
K	N	E	Q	A	W	D	L	H	U	E	T	N	A	C	A	V	U	Q
A	I	J	N	M	R	V	Y	F	U	N	L	U	V	B	E	F	C	S
Y	A	Z	F	P	Z	E	A	L	G	N	D	S	S	R	M	E	S	A

ACQUIRED	CURIOUS	MARQUEE	RAUCOUS
ALLEGIANCE	DEVASTATION	MASSACRE	REVEL
ANTIC	DISPARAGED	MERGE	SHUN
APPLAUD	DORMANT	MERINGUE	SUBDUED
ASPHALT	ELUSIVE	MESA	SULLEN
BAFFLE	GAPED	MULL	SWOON
BARREN	HESITATE	ORATORICAL	TRANCE
BLITHELY	HOAX	PARANOID	UKULELE
CACTI	IMPULSE	PERPETUAL	VACANT
CONFOUND	LOTUS	PRONE	VAMP
CONVINCED	MANIA	RAPTURE	ZEAL

Stargirl Vocabulary Word Search 3 Answer Key

Words are placed backwards, forward, diagonally, up and down. Words listed below are included in the maze. Circle the hidden vocabulary words in the maze.

D U A L P P A M A S S A C R E X C P D
I A U S S W E A A B U E E
S C O K U O P S P O E L R P V
P Q R U O B L H T H L I E A
A U A N L U D U A U T E S
R I M T P E R U L S H O T
A R M O E R E A T H I E V A
G E T I C R E L D E V S T
E D N M N O I L F C S E L I
D A E N M E C F N I T O
P M R C R V G E A R T C M S N
P A R A N O I D A R B L M A R Q U E E
A A O O C A N N T P G C T U L L
B M D I N C F G L E E E L C O
A T C V E E S O U O D E O E
N E A D H U E T N A C A V U
A I M U N U E S
A P Z E A L N D S R M E S A

ACQUIRED   CURIOUS   MARQUEE   RAUCOUS

ALLEGIANCE   DEVASTATION   MASSACRE   REVEL

ANTIC   DISPARAGED   MERGE   SHUN

APPLAUD   DORMANT   MERINGUE   SUBDUED

ASPHALT   ELUSIVE   MESA   SULLEN

BAFFLE   GAPED   MULL   SWOON

BARREN   HESITATE   ORATORICAL   TRANCE

BLITHELY   HOAX   PARANOID   UKULELE

CACTI   IMPULSE   PERPETUAL   VACANT

CONFOUND   LOTUS   PRONE   VAMP

CONVINCED   MANIA   RAPTURE   ZEAL

Stargirl Vocabulary Word Search 4

Words are placed backwards, forward, diagonally, up and down. Words listed below are included in the maze. Circle the hidden vocabulary words in the maze.

O	B	L	I	V	I	O	U	S	T	R	A	P	T	U	R	E	C	P
A	P	P	L	A	U	D	K	P	X	S	N	H	E	S	G	S	O	J
T	R	A	N	C	E	L	U	V	E	F	Q	N	C	R	C	L	N	B
H	O	A	X	A	P	I	L	M	V	S	O	I	E	D	U	U	F	V
P	Y	P	B	N	D	N	E	Q	Q	R	T	M	L	L	R	P	O	V
G	G	A	K	T	V	G	L	E	P	A	F	J	S	G	I	M	U	Y
M	A	R	Q	U	E	E	E	T	N	H	A	R	A	E	O	I	N	Q
E	C	A	Y	D	O	R	M	A	N	T	C	P	Z	L	U	V	D	S
R	Q	N	S	K	W	E	F	G	Y	N	E	P	A	F	S	A	G	M
I	U	O	F	P	P	R	K	O	E	D	T	C	G	F	M	M	D	S
N	I	I	Z	I	H	X	L	R	G	C	I	S	S	A	C	P	E	P
G	R	D	S	W	T	A	R	R	R	R	O	C	U	B	N	L	C	Z
U	E	O	T	S	B	A	L	E	O	C	U	R	A	L	E	T	N	Z
E	D	E	U	D	B	U	S	T	N	M	S	X	E	C	L	S	I	G
E	R	R	A	Z	I	B	A	N	C	U	L	W	S	V	T	E	V	C
T	K	C	X	D	E	R	C	I	T	L	Y	O	O	H	E	I	N	D
M	A	N	I	A	O	A	H	O	D	L	S	T	K	O	U	L	O	D
V	E	E	R	E	D	E	L	U	S	I	V	E	P	B	N	N	C	W

ACQUIRED	ELUSIVE	MARQUEE	SUBDUED
ANTIC	EPISODE	MERGE	SULLEN
APPLAUD	FACETIOUSLY	MERINGUE	SWOON
ASPHALT	FANATICS	MESA	TRANCE
BAFFLE	GAPED	MULL	UKULELE
BARREN	HOAX	OBLIVIOUS	VACANT
BIZARRE	IMPULSE	ORATORICAL	VAMP
CACTI	INTERROGATE	PARANOID	VEERED
CONFOUND	ISOSCELES	PRONE	ZEAL
CONVINCED	LINGER	RAPTURE	
CURIOUS	LOTUS	REVEL	
DORMANT	MANIA	SHUN	

Stargirl Vocabulary Word Search 4 Answer Key

Words are placed backwards, forward, diagonally, up and down. Words listed below are included in the maze. Circle the hidden vocabulary words in the maze.

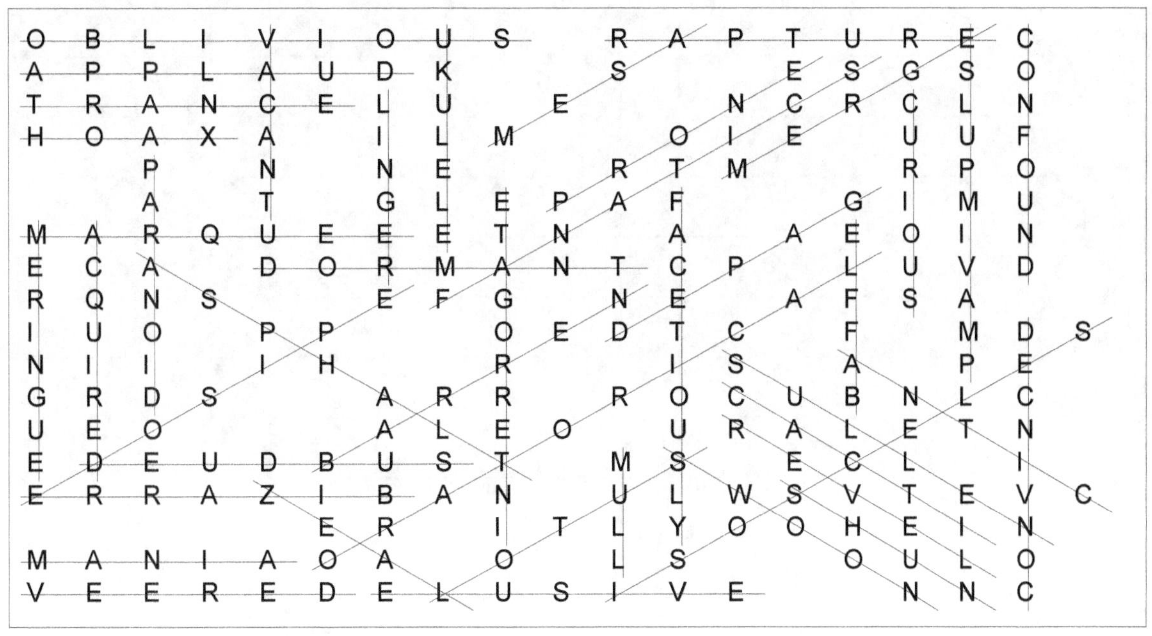

ACQUIRED	ELUSIVE	MARQUEE	SUBDUED
ANTIC	EPISODE	MERGE	SULLEN
APPLAUD	FACETIOUSLY	MERINGUE	SWOON
ASPHALT	FANATICS	MESA	TRANCE
BAFFLE	GAPED	MULL	UKULELE
BARREN	HOAX	OBLIVIOUS	VACANT
BIZARRE	IMPULSE	ORATORICAL	VAMP
CACTI	INTERROGATE	PARANOID	VEERED
CONFOUND	ISOSCELES	PRONE	ZEAL
CONVINCED	LINGER	RAPTURE	
CURIOUS	LOTUS	REVEL	
DORMANT	MANIA	SHUN	

Stargirl Vocabulary Crossword 1

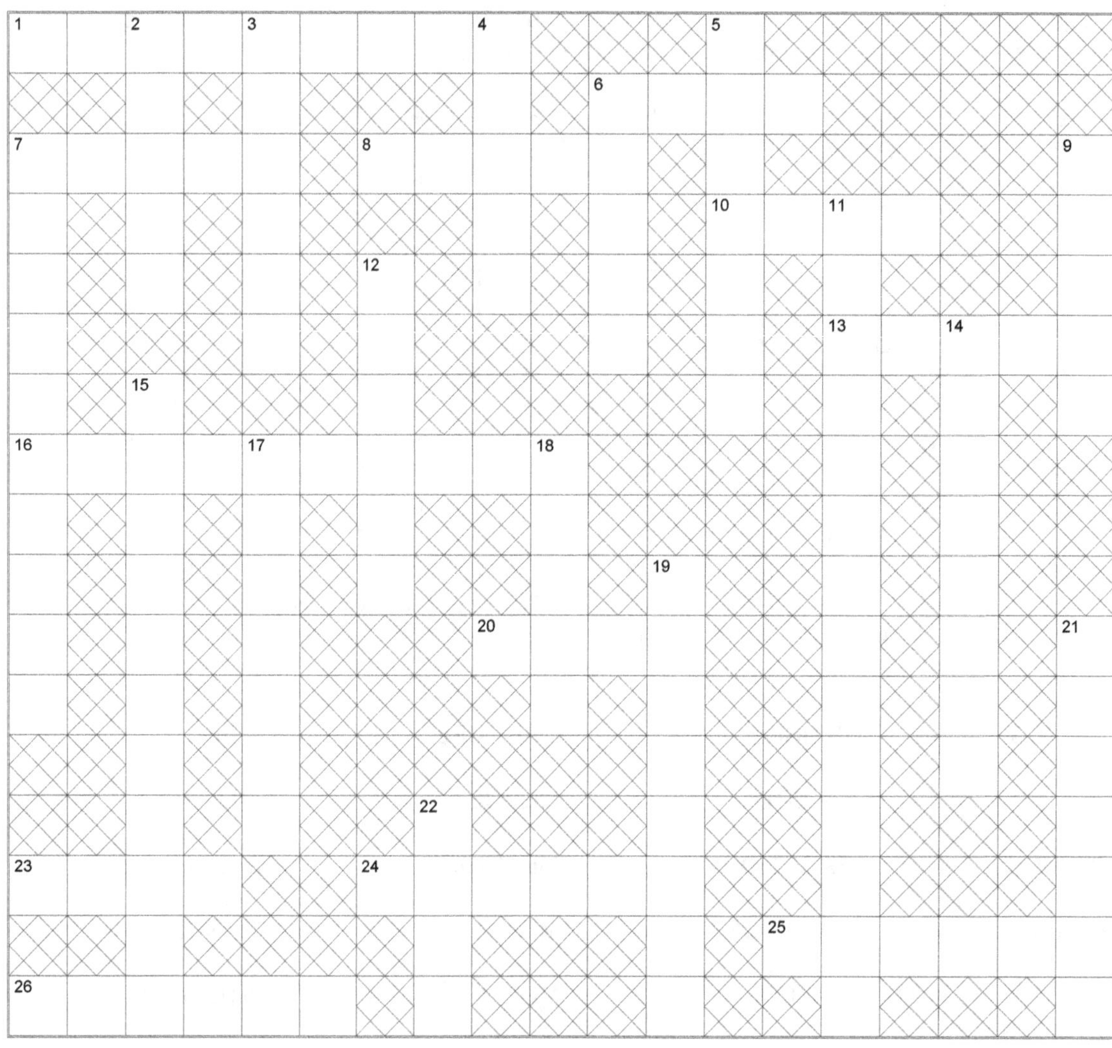

Across

1. Unaware
6. Consider mentally
7. Extravagant act or gesture
8. Lying face down
10. To avoid deliberately and consistently
13. Plural of cactus
16. Approaching the same point from different directions
20. Enthusiasm
23. Deceitful prank
24. Frustrate; puzzle
25. Without vegetation
26. Turned

Down

2. Sitting cross-legged with the feet above the thighs
3. Empty
4. Faint
5. Can't be caught
6. Join together
7. To be thankful or show gratitude for
9. Craze; excessively popular thing to do
11. Out of the ordinary; unusual
12. Tarry; wait around
14. To cause to become confused
15. Question
17. Incident; event
18. Stared at wonderingly as with the mouth wide open
19. Cheerful; carefree
21. Asleep; not active
22. Unscrupulously seductive woman

Stargirl Vocabulary Crossword 1 Answer Key

<table>
<tr><td>1 O</td><td>B</td><td>2 L</td><td>I</td><td>3 V</td><td>I</td><td>O</td><td>U</td><td>4 S</td><td></td><td></td><td></td><td>5 E</td><td></td><td></td><td></td><td></td><td></td><td></td></tr>
<tr><td></td><td></td><td>O</td><td></td><td>A</td><td></td><td></td><td></td><td>W</td><td></td><td>6 M</td><td>U</td><td>L</td><td>L</td><td></td><td></td><td></td><td></td><td></td></tr>
<tr><td>7 A</td><td>N</td><td>T</td><td>I</td><td>C</td><td></td><td>8 P</td><td>R</td><td>O</td><td>N</td><td>E</td><td></td><td>U</td><td></td><td></td><td></td><td></td><td></td><td>9 M</td></tr>
<tr><td>P</td><td></td><td>U</td><td></td><td>A</td><td></td><td></td><td></td><td>O</td><td></td><td>R</td><td></td><td>10 S</td><td>H</td><td>11 U</td><td>N</td><td></td><td></td><td>A</td></tr>
<tr><td>P</td><td></td><td>S</td><td></td><td>N</td><td></td><td>12 L</td><td></td><td>N</td><td></td><td>G</td><td></td><td>I</td><td></td><td>N</td><td></td><td></td><td></td><td>N</td></tr>
<tr><td>R</td><td></td><td></td><td></td><td>T</td><td></td><td>I</td><td></td><td></td><td></td><td>E</td><td></td><td>V</td><td></td><td>13 C</td><td>A</td><td>14 C</td><td>T</td><td>I</td></tr>
<tr><td>E</td><td></td><td>15 I</td><td></td><td></td><td></td><td>N</td><td></td><td></td><td></td><td></td><td></td><td>E</td><td></td><td>O</td><td></td><td>O</td><td></td><td>A</td></tr>
<tr><td>16 C</td><td>O</td><td>N</td><td>V</td><td>17 E</td><td>R</td><td>G</td><td>I</td><td>N</td><td>18 G</td><td></td><td></td><td></td><td></td><td>M</td><td></td><td>N</td><td></td><td></td></tr>
<tr><td>I</td><td></td><td>T</td><td></td><td>P</td><td></td><td>E</td><td></td><td></td><td>A</td><td></td><td></td><td></td><td></td><td>M</td><td></td><td>F</td><td></td><td></td></tr>
<tr><td>A</td><td></td><td>E</td><td></td><td>I</td><td></td><td>R</td><td></td><td></td><td>P</td><td></td><td>19 B</td><td></td><td></td><td>O</td><td></td><td>O</td><td></td><td></td></tr>
<tr><td>T</td><td></td><td>R</td><td></td><td>S</td><td></td><td></td><td></td><td>20 Z</td><td>E</td><td>A</td><td>L</td><td></td><td></td><td>N</td><td></td><td>U</td><td></td><td>21 D</td></tr>
<tr><td>E</td><td></td><td>R</td><td></td><td>O</td><td></td><td></td><td></td><td></td><td>D</td><td></td><td>I</td><td></td><td></td><td></td><td></td><td>N</td><td></td><td>O</td></tr>
<tr><td></td><td></td><td>O</td><td></td><td>D</td><td></td><td></td><td></td><td></td><td></td><td></td><td>T</td><td></td><td></td><td></td><td></td><td>D</td><td></td><td>R</td></tr>
<tr><td></td><td></td><td>G</td><td></td><td>E</td><td></td><td></td><td>22 V</td><td></td><td></td><td></td><td>H</td><td></td><td></td><td></td><td></td><td></td><td></td><td>M</td></tr>
<tr><td>23 H</td><td>O</td><td>A</td><td>X</td><td></td><td></td><td>24 B</td><td>A</td><td>F</td><td>F</td><td>L</td><td>E</td><td></td><td></td><td></td><td></td><td></td><td></td><td>A</td></tr>
<tr><td></td><td></td><td>T</td><td></td><td></td><td></td><td></td><td>M</td><td></td><td></td><td></td><td></td><td></td><td>25 B</td><td>A</td><td>R</td><td>R</td><td>E</td><td>N</td></tr>
<tr><td>26 V</td><td>E</td><td>E</td><td>R</td><td>E</td><td>D</td><td></td><td>P</td><td></td><td></td><td></td><td></td><td></td><td></td><td></td><td></td><td></td><td></td><td>T</td></tr>
</table>

Across

1. Unaware
6. Consider mentally
7. Extravagant act or gesture
8. Lying face down
10. To avoid deliberately and consistently
13. Plural of cactus
16. Approaching the same point from different directions
20. Enthusiasm
23. Deceitful prank
24. Frustrate; puzzle
25. Without vegetation
26. Turned

Down

2. Sitting cross-legged with the feet above the thighs
3. Empty
4. Faint
5. Can't be caught
6. Join together
7. To be thankful or show gratitude for
9. Craze; excessively popular thing to do
11. Out of the ordinary; unusual
12. Tarry; wait around
14. To cause to become confused
15. Question
17. Incident; event
18. Stared at wonderingly as with the mouth wide open
19. Cheerful; carefree
21. Asleep; not active
22. Unscrupulously seductive woman

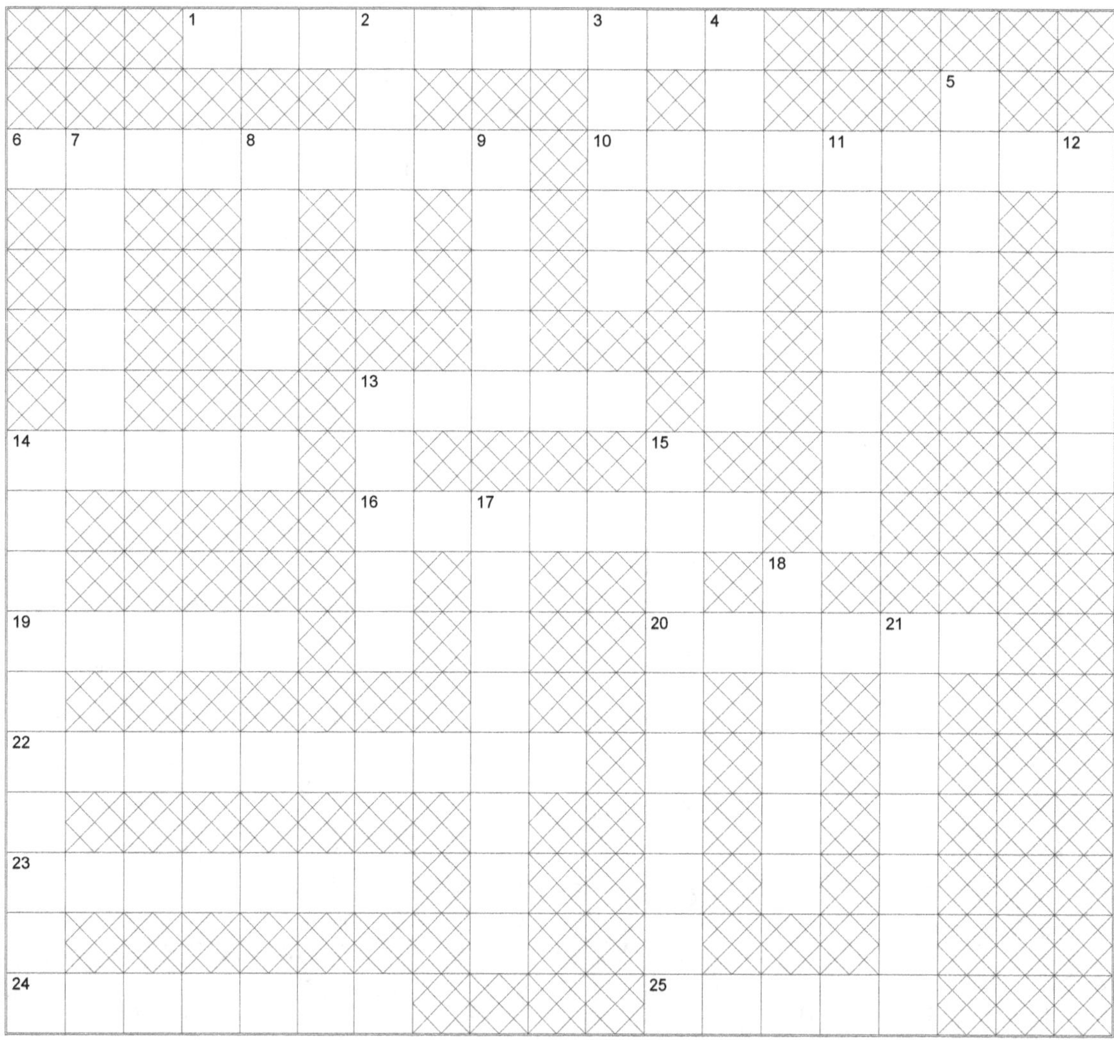

Across

1. Belittled
6. Unaware
10. Lasting for eternity
13. Craze; excessively popular thing to do
14. Extravagant act or gesture
16. Ecstasy; the state of being transported by a lofty emotion
19. To take great pleasure or delight
20. A state of detachment from one's physical surroundings
22. Approaching the same point from different directions
23. Express approval by clapping hands
24. Incident; event
25. Sitting cross-legged with the feet above the thighs

Down

2. Lying face down
3. Stared at wonderingly as with the mouth wide open
4. Asleep; not active
5. Consider mentally
7. Without vegetation
8. Unscrupulously seductive woman
9. Faint
11. Can't be caught
12. Tarry; wait around
13. Join together
14. To be thankful or show gratitude for
15. Related to public speaking
17. Showing unreasonable distrust or suspicion
18. Frustrate; puzzle
21. Eager to acquire knowledge

Stargirl Vocabulary Crossword 2 Answer Key

Across

1. Belittled
6. Unaware
10. Lasting for eternity
13. Craze; excessively popular thing to do
14. Extravagant act or gesture
16. Ecstasy; the state of being transported by a lofty emotion
19. To take great pleasure or delight
20. A state of detachment from one's physical surroundings
22. Approaching the same point from different directions
23. Express approval by clapping hands
24. Incident; event
25. Sitting cross-legged with the feet above the thighs

Down

2. Lying face down
3. Stared at wonderingly as with the mouth wide open
4. Asleep; not active
5. Consider mentally
7. Without vegetation
8. Unscrupulously seductive woman
9. Faint
11. Can't be caught
12. Tarry; wait around
13. Join together
14. To be thankful or show gratitude for
15. Related to public speaking
17. Showing unreasonable distrust or suspicion
18. Frustrate; puzzle
21. Eager to acquire knowledge

Stargirl Vocabulary Crossword 3

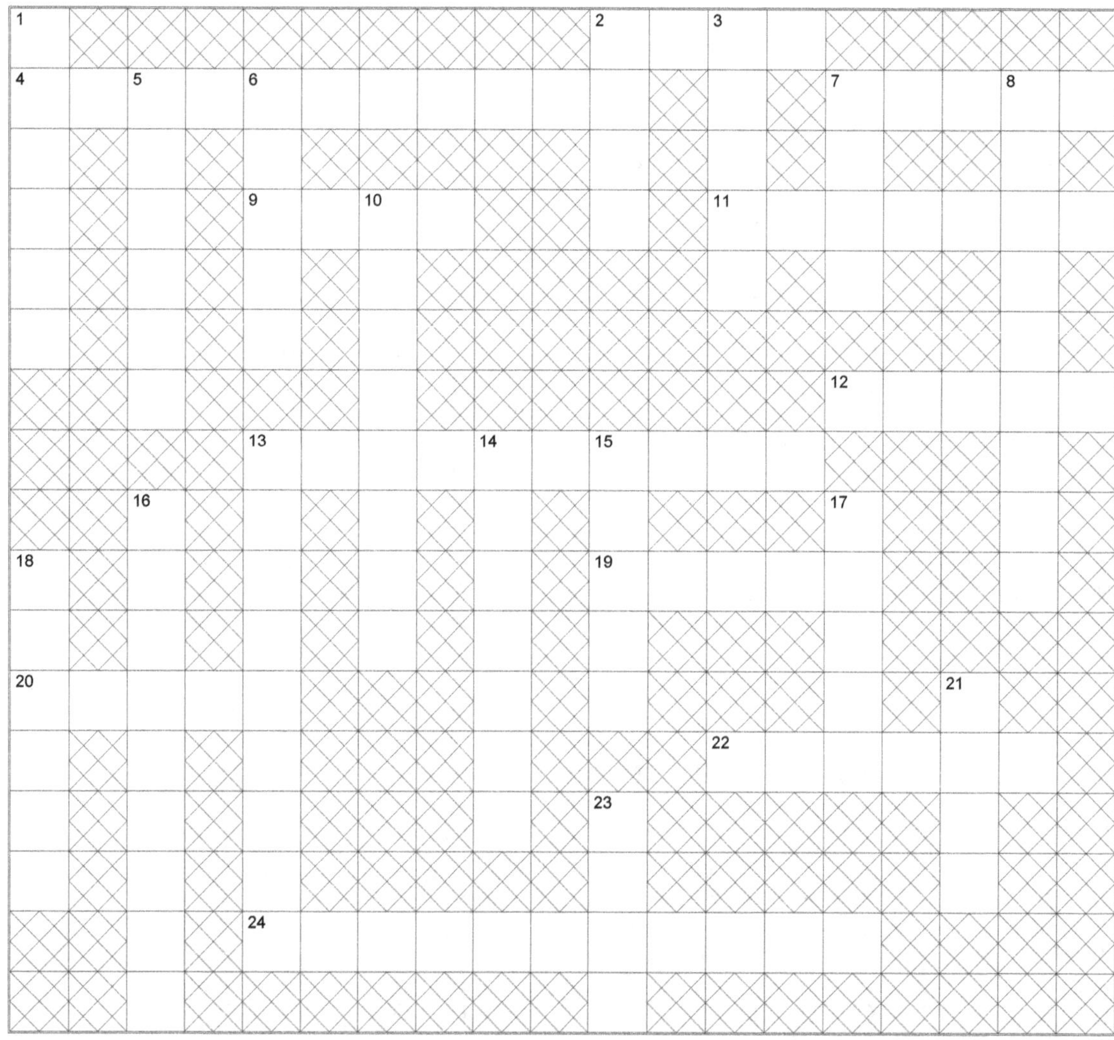

Across

2. Consider mentally
4. Question
7. Faint
9. Unscrupulously seductive woman
11. A small four-stringed guitar
12. Extravagant act or gesture
13. Approaching the same point from different directions
19. Lying face down
20. Plural of cactus
22. Turned
24. Destruction

Down

1. Tarry; wait around
2. Flat-topped elevation with one or more clifflike sides
3. Sitting cross-legged with the feet above the thighs
5. A state of detachment from one's physical surroundings
6. To take great pleasure or delight
7. To avoid deliberately and consistently
8. Unaware
10. Fluffy pastry topping made of beaten eggs
13. Caused to believe something
14. Can't be caught
15. Stared at wonderingly as with the mouth wide open
16. Thought up; imagined
17. Join together
18. Empty
21. Enthusiasm
23. Deceitful prank

Across

2. Consider mentally
4. Question
7. Faint
9. Unscrupulously seductive woman
11. A small four-stringed guitar
12. Extravagant act or gesture
13. Approaching the same point from different directions
19. Lying face down
20. Plural of cactus
22. Turned
24. Destruction

Down

1. Tarry; wait around
2. Flat-topped elevation with one or more clifflike sides
3. Sitting cross-legged with the feet above the thighs
5. A state of detachment from one's physical surroundings
6. To take great pleasure or delight
7. To avoid deliberately and consistently
8. Unaware
10. Fluffy pastry topping made of beaten eggs
13. Caused to believe something
14. Can't be caught
15. Stared at wonderingly as with the mouth wide open
16. Thought up; imagined
17. Join together
18. Empty
21. Enthusiasm
23. Deceitful prank

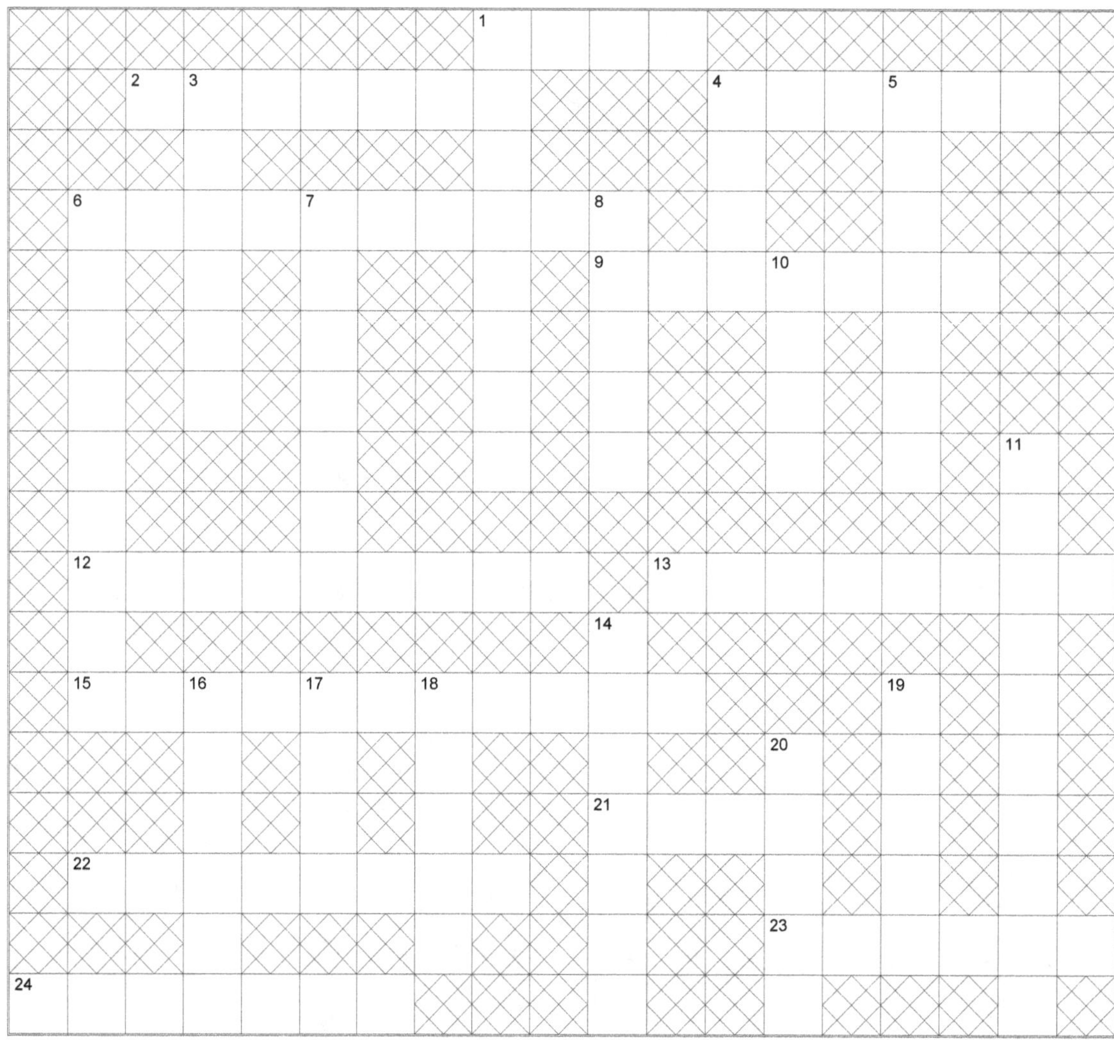

Across

1. Consider mentally
2. Can't be caught
4. Empty
6. Approaching the same point from different directions
9. Pavement
12. Thought up; imagined
13. Cheerful; carefree
15. Destruction
21. Flat-topped elevation with one or more clifflike sides
22. Showing unreasonable distrust or suspicion
23. A state of detachment from one's physical surroundings
24. Calmed; quieted
.

Down

1. Fluffy pastry topping made of beaten eggs
3. Tarry; wait around
4. Unscrupulously seductive woman
5. Express approval by clapping hands
6. Caused to believe something
7. Incident; event
8. Stared at wonderingly as with the mouth wide open
10. Deceitful prank
11. Loyalty
14. Asleep; not active
16. Turned
17. To avoid deliberately and consistently
18. Extravagant act or gesture
19. Craze; excessively popular thing to do
20. Plural of cactus

Stargirl Vocabulary Crossword 4 Answer Key

							¹M	U	L	L			⁴V	A	C	⁵A	N	T	
²E	L	³U	S	I	V	E							A			P			
	I					R							A			P			
⁶C	O	N	V	⁷E	R	G	I	N	⁸G		M			P					
O		G		P				N	⁹A	S	P	¹⁰H	A	L	T				
N		E		I				G	P			O		A					
V		R		S				U	E			A		U					
I				O				E	D			X		D		¹¹A			
N				D												L			
¹²C	O	N	C	E	I	V	E	D		¹³B	L	I	T	H	E	L	Y		
E									¹⁴D							E			
¹⁵D	¹⁶E	¹⁷V	A	¹⁸S	T	A	T	I	O	N			¹⁹M		G				
	E		H		N				R		²⁰C		A		I				
	E		U		T			²¹M	E	S	A		N		A				
²²P	A	R	A	N	O	I	D		A		C		I		N				
	E				C				N		²³T	R	A	N	C	E			
²⁴S	U	B	D	U	E	D			T		I				E				

Across

1. Consider mentally
2. Can't be caught
4. Empty
6. Approaching the same point from different directions
9. Pavement
12. Thought up; imagined
13. Cheerful; carefree
15. Destruction
21. Flat-topped elevation with one or more clifflike sides
22. Showing unreasonable distrust or suspicion
23. A state of detachment from one's physical surroundings
24. Calmed; quieted

Down

1. Fluffy pastry topping made of beaten eggs
3. Tarry; wait around
4. Unscrupulously seductive woman
5. Express approval by clapping hands
6. Caused to believe something
7. Incident; event
8. Stared at wonderingly as with the mouth wide open
10. Deceitful prank
11. Loyalty
14. Asleep; not active
16. Turned
17. To avoid deliberately and consistently
18. Extravagant act or gesture
19. Craze; excessively popular thing to do
20. Plural of cactus

Stargirl Vocabulary Juggle Letters 1

1. UPLAPAD   = 1. ______________________
                     Express approval by clapping hands

2. GLRNEI   = 2. ______________________
                     Tarry; wait around

3. THLYLEBI   = 3. ______________________
                     Cheerful; carefree

4. EQDIUCAR   = 4. ______________________
                     Got

5. AHEIETST   = 5. ______________________
                     Hold back in uncertainty

6. EUEINMGR   = 6. ______________________
                     Fluffy pastry topping made of beaten eggs

7. IRDNOAAP   = 7. ______________________
                     Showing unreasonable distrust or suspicion

8. NWOOS   = 8. ______________________
                     Faint

9. ERZRIBA   = 9. ______________________
                     Strikingly unconventional; odd

10. DOINEECCV   =10. ______________________
                     Thought up; imagined

11. AUUCROS   =11. ______________________
                     Noisy; boisterous

12. SMEA   =12. ______________________
                     Flat-topped elevation with one or more clifflike sides

13. TNCIASFA   =13. ______________________
                     People possessed by an excessive enthusiasm for
                     something

14. IENONCCVD   =14. ______________________
                     Caused to believe something

15. TEPAEPRLU   =15. ______________________
                     Lasting for eternity

1. UPLAPAD

= 1. APPLAUD
Express approval by clapping hands

2. GLRNEI

= 2. LINGER
Tarry; wait around

3. THLYLEBI

= 3. BLITHELY
Cheerful; carefree

4. EQDIUCAR

= 4. ACQUIRED
Got

5. AHEIETST

= 5. HESITATE
Hold back in uncertainty

6. EUEINMGR

= 6. MERINGUE
Fluffy pastry topping made of beaten eggs

7. IRDNOAAP

= 7. PARANOID
Showing unreasonable distrust or suspicion

8. NWOOS

= 8. SWOON
Faint

9. ERZRIBA

= 9. BIZARRE
Strikingly unconventional; odd

10. DOINEECCV

=10. CONCEIVED
Thought up; imagined

11. AUUCROS

=11. RAUCOUS
Noisy; boisterous

12. SMEA

=12. MESA
Flat-topped elevation with one or more clifflike sides

13. TNCIASFA

=13. FANATICS
People possessed by an excessive enthusiasm for something

14. IENONCCVD

=14. CONVINCED
Caused to believe something

15. TEPAEPRLU

=15. PERPETUAL
Lasting for eternity

Stargirl Vocabulary Juggle Letters 2

1. LISVUIOOB   = 1. ___________________________
                      Unaware

2. HSUN   = 2. ___________________________
                      To avoid deliberately and consistently

3. ONASVAIDTTE   = 3. ___________________________
                      Destruction

4. VNAOOLTNINEUCN   = 4. ___________________________
                      Out of the ordinary; unusual

5. AXOH   = 5. ___________________________
                      Deceitful prank

6. EPDISOE   = 6. ___________________________
                      Incident; event

7. DGSERAADIP   = 7. ___________________________
                      Belittled

8. AFLBFE   = 8. ___________________________
                      Frustrate; puzzle

9. PUIACNIML   = 9. ___________________________
                      City

10. NVNCCDEOI   =10. ___________________________
                      Caused to believe something

11. TAANSFIC   =11. ___________________________
                      People possessed by an excessive enthusiasm for
                      something

12. QEURMAE   =12. ___________________________
                      Signboard projecting over an entrance to a building

13. CEANILAEGL   =13. ___________________________
                      Loyalty

14. LAPPUDA   =14. ___________________________
                      Express approval by clapping hands

15. EOTYSLAFUCI   =15. ___________________________
                      In fun; as a joke

1. LISVUIOOB

= 1. OBLIVIOUS

Unaware

2. HSUN

= 2. SHUN

To avoid deliberately and consistently

3. ONASVAIDTTE

= 3. DEVASTATION

Destruction

4. VNAOOLTNINEUCN

= 4. UNCONVENTIONAL

Out of the ordinary; unusual

5. AXOH

= 5. HOAX

Deceitful prank

6. EPDISOE

= 6. EPISODE

Incident; event

7. DGSERAADIP

= 7. DISPARAGED

Belittled

8. AFLBFE

= 8. BAFFLE

Frustrate; puzzle

9. PUIACNIML

= 9. MUNICIPAL

City

10. NVNCCDEOI

=10. CONVINCED

Caused to believe something

11. TAANSFIC

=11. FANATICS

People possessed by an excessive enthusiasm for something

12. QEURMAE

=12. MARQUEE

Signboard projecting over an entrance to a building

13. CEANILAEGL

=13. ALLEGIANCE

Loyalty

14. LAPPUDA

=14. APPLAUD

Express approval by clapping hands

15. EOTYSLAFUCI

=15. FACETIOUSLY

In fun; as a joke

1. EEVLSUI   = 1. ___________________________
Can't be caught

2. ENLLUS   = 2. ___________________________
Brooding; gloomy

3. SETEDRIPS   = 3. ___________________________
Held firmly to some purpose or undertaking despite obstacles or setbacks

4. EQURAEM   = 4. ___________________________
Signboard projecting over an entrance to a building

5. LRORCTAOIA   = 5. ___________________________
Related to public speaking

6. ATNVCA   = 6. ___________________________
Empty

7. ESITATHE   = 7. ___________________________
Hold back in uncertainty

8. ERBNAR   = 8. ___________________________
Without vegetation

9. ERZRBIA   = 9. ___________________________
Strikingly unconventional; odd

10. PSTALHA   =10. ___________________________
Pavement

11. SEPADADIGR   =11. ___________________________
Belittled

12. ONSWO   =12. ___________________________
Faint

13. BDUDUES   =13. ___________________________
Calmed; quieted

14. NESDDREEA   =14. ___________________________
Gave a musical performance, especially one for a sweetheart

15. EOPIDSE   =15. ___________________________
Incident; event

1. EEVLSUI

= 1. ELUSIVE

Can't be caught

2. ENLLUS

= 2. SULLEN

Brooding; gloomy

3. SETEDRIPS

= 3. PERSISTED

Held firmly to some purpose or undertaking despite obstacles or setbacks

4. EQURAEM

= 4. MARQUEE

Signboard projecting over an entrance to a building

5. LRORCTAOIA

= 5. ORATORICAL

Related to public speaking

6. ATNVCA

= 6. VACANT

Empty

7. ESITATHE

= 7. HESITATE

Hold back in uncertainty

8. ERBNAR

= 8. BARREN

Without vegetation

9. ERZRBIA

= 9. BIZARRE

Strikingly unconventional; odd

10. PSTALHA

=10. ASPHALT

Pavement

11. SEPADADIGR

=11. DISPARAGED

Belittled

12. ONSWO

=12. SWOON

Faint

13. BDUDUES

=13. SUBDUED

Calmed; quieted

14. NESDDREEA

=14. SERENADED

Gave a musical performance, especially one for a sweetheart

15. EOPIDSE

=15. EPISODE

Incident; event

Stargirl Vocabulary Juggle Letters 4

1. DSTIYABUR = 1. ___________________________

Something that is ridiculous or unreasonable

2. TEIAHTES = 2. ___________________________

Hold back in uncertainty

3. AOUUSRC = 3. ___________________________

Noisy; boisterous

4. EMSA = 4. ___________________________

Flat-topped elevation with one or more clifflike sides

5. LULM = 5. ___________________________

Consider mentally

6. IERSAPDDGA = 6. ___________________________

Belittled

7. RATAIEEPPC = 7. ___________________________

To be thankful or show gratitude for

8. VTASITADOEN = 8. ___________________________

Destruction

9. ESDIPTERS = 9. ___________________________

Held firmly to some purpose or undertaking despite obstacles or setbacks

10. PAUADLP =10. ___________________________

Express approval by clapping hands

11. ROTGNTEEAIR =11. ___________________________

Question

12. TLNTAETIYEV =12. ___________________________

Uncertainly; experimentally

13. LNELSU =13. ___________________________

Brooding; gloomy

14. EIAGLACNLE =14. ___________________________

Loyalty

15. SLCSEOSEI =15. ___________________________

Having two equal sides

1. DSTIYABUR	= 1. ABSURDITY
	Something that is ridiculous or unreasonable
2. TEIAHTES	= 2. HESITATE
	Hold back in uncertainty
3. AOUUSRC	= 3. RAUCOUS
	Noisy; boisterous
4. EMSA	= 4. MESA
	Flat-topped elevation with one or more clifflike sides
5. LULM	= 5. MULL
	Consider mentally
6. IERSAPDDGA	= 6. DISPARAGED
	Belittled
7. RATAIEEPPC	= 7. APPRECIATE
	To be thankful or show gratitude for
8. VTASITADOEN	= 8. DEVASTATION
	Destruction
9. ESDIPTERS	= 9. PERSISTED
	Held firmly to some purpose or undertaking despite obstacles or setbacks
10. PAUADLP	=10. APPLAUD
	Express approval by clapping hands
11. ROTGNTEEAIR	=11. INTERROGATE
	Question
12. TLNTAETIYEV	=12. TENTATIVELY
	Uncertainly; experimentally
13. LNELSU	=13. SULLEN
	Brooding; gloomy
14. EIAGLACNLE	=14. ALLEGIANCE
	Loyalty
15. SLCSEOSEI	=15. ISOSCELES
	Having two equal sides

ABSURDITY	Something that is ridiculous or unreasonable
ACQUIRED	Got
ALLEGIANCE	Loyalty
ANTIC	Extravagant act or gesture
APPLAUD	Express approval by clapping hands
APPRECIATE	To be thankful or show gratitude for

ASPHALT	Pavement
BAFFLE	Frustrate; puzzle
BARREN	Without vegetation
BIZARRE	Strikingly unconventional; odd
BLITHELY	Cheerful; carefree
CACTI	Plural of cactus

CONCEIVED	Thought up; imagined
CONFOUND	To cause to become confused
CONVERGING	Approaching the same point from different directions
CONVINCED	Caused to believe something
CURIOUS	Eager to acquire knowledge
DEVASTATION	Destruction

DISPARAGED	Belittled
DORMANT	Asleep; not active
ELUSIVE	Can't be caught
EPISODE	Incident; event
FACETIOUSLY	In fun; as a joke
FANATICS	People possessed by an excessive enthusiasm for something

GAPED	Stared at wonderingly as with the mouth wide open
HESITATE	Hold back in uncertainty
HOAX	Deceitful prank
IMPULSE	Urge
INTERROGATE	Question
ISOSCELES	Having two equal sides

LINGER	Tarry; wait around
LOTUS	Sitting cross-legged with the feet above the thighs
MANIA	Craze; excessively popular thing to do
MARQUEE	Signboard projecting over an entrance to a building
MASSACRE	Slaughter
MERGE	Join together

MERINGUE	Fluffy pastry topping made of beaten eggs
MESA	Flat-topped elevation with one or more clifflike sides
MULL	Consider mentally
MUNICIPAL	City
NONCONFORMITY	Refusing to be bound by the accepted rules or practices of a group
OBLIVIOUS	Unaware

ORATORICAL	Related to public speaking
PARANOID	Showing unreasonable distrust or suspicion
PERPETUAL	Lasting for eternity
PERSISTED	Held firmly to some purpose or undertaking despite obstacles or setbacks
PRONE	Lying face down
RAPTURE	Ecstasy; the state of being transported by a lofty emotion

RAUCOUS	Noisy; boisterous
REVEL	To take great pleasure or delight
SERENADED	Gave a musical performance, especially one for a sweetheart
SHUN	To avoid deliberately and consistently
SUBDUED	Calmed; quieted
SULLEN	Brooding; gloomy

SWOON	Faint
TENTATIVELY	Uncertainly; experimentally
TRANCE	A state of detachment from one's physical surroundings
UKULELE	A small four-stringed guitar
UNCONVENTIONAL	Out of the ordinary; unusual
VACANT	Empty

VAMP	Unscrupulously seductive woman
VEERED	Turned
ZEAL	Enthusiasm

Stargirl Vocabulary

TENTATIVELY	NONCONFORMITY	PARANOID	DORMANT	ZEAL
MUNICIPAL	CONCEIVED	DISPARAGED	PRONE	ABSURDITY
SHUN	ORATORICAL	FREE SPACE	VACANT	SULLEN
ALLEGIANCE	CACTI	SWOON	CONVINCED	ANTIC
SUBDUED	OBLIVIOUS	INTERROGATE	ASPHALT	HESITATE

Stargirl Vocabulary

PERSISTED	UNCONVENTIONAL	RAPTURE	PERPETUAL	SERENADED
RAUCOUS	BIZARRE	MARQUEE	REVEL	EPISODE
ISOSCELES	VEERED	FREE SPACE	BAFFLE	IMPULSE
CONVERGING	CONFOUND	DEVASTATION	MANIA	BARREN
LOTUS	MERGE	UKULELE	VAMP	MASSACRE

Stargirl Vocabulary

PRONE	MANIA	UKULELE	MUNICIPAL	DEVASTATION
PARANOID	ASPHALT	VEERED	CURIOUS	PERSISTED
BIZARRE	SULLEN	FREE SPACE	ISOSCELES	VAMP
VACANT	CONVINCED	MERGE	APPRECIATE	MESA
ACQUIRED	MASSACRE	MULL	CACTI	INTERROGATE

Stargirl Vocabulary

BARREN	PERPETUAL	LOTUS	MERINGUE	FANATICS
TENTATIVELY	MARQUEE	ALLEGIANCE	HESITATE	RAPTURE
APPLAUD	DORMANT	FREE SPACE	BLITHELY	RAUCOUS
CONFOUND	CONVERGING	OBLIVIOUS	SUBDUED	REVEL
SERENADED	EPISODE	BAFFLE	CONCEIVED	ORATORICAL

Stargirl Vocabulary

VAMP	MASSACRE	MULL	APPRECIATE	CONFOUND
TRANCE	ACQUIRED	MANIA	BARREN	LOTUS
RAUCOUS	NONCONFORMITY	FREE SPACE	FACETIOUSLY	FANATICS
SERENADED	MUNICIPAL	CONVINCED	RAPTURE	SULLEN
ELUSIVE	ALLEGIANCE	VEERED	HOAX	PERPETUAL

Stargirl Vocabulary

HESITATE	OBLIVIOUS	SHUN	ABSURDITY	BAFFLE
ISOSCELES	APPLAUD	CURIOUS	BIZARRE	SWOON
GAPED	CONVERGING	FREE SPACE	DEVASTATION	DORMANT
UKULELE	IMPULSE	INTERROGATE	MERINGUE	CACTI
DISPARAGED	MESA	UNCONVENTIONAL	TENTATIVELY	PARANOID

UKULELE	BLITHELY	DEVASTATION	CONCEIVED	SERENADED
FANATICS	CONFOUND	MARQUEE	APPLAUD	OBLIVIOUS
CACTI	ACQUIRED	FREE SPACE	GAPED	MERINGUE
LINGER	MULL	BAFFLE	SHUN	ABSURDITY
TENTATIVELY	ALLEGIANCE	ELUSIVE	CONVERGING	MUNICIPAL

Stargirl Vocabulary

DORMANT	ASPHALT	VAMP	PARANOID	SUBDUED
UNCONVENTIONAL	INTERROGATE	FACETIOUSLY	IMPULSE	ANTIC
BARREN	EPISODE	FREE SPACE	REVEL	RAPTURE
ISOSCELES	LOTUS	HESITATE	MASSACRE	VEERED
DISPARAGED	TRANCE	RAUCOUS	PERSISTED	MANIA

Stargirl Vocabulary

CACTI	ISOSCELES	EPISODE	MESA	LOTUS
ANTIC	CONFOUND	LINGER	SHUN	PARANOID
FACETIOUSLY	BAFFLE	FREE SPACE	CURIOUS	MERINGUE
DORMANT	BLITHELY	ORATORICAL	SULLEN	IMPULSE
DEVASTATION	CONCEIVED	UNCONVENTIONAL	REVEL	HOAX

Stargirl Vocabulary

PERSISTED	FANATICS	MULL	ABSURDITY	VAMP
HESITATE	ALLEGIANCE	TENTATIVELY	SWOON	BIZARRE
MANIA	ZEAL	FREE SPACE	ACQUIRED	APPLAUD
CONVERGING	DISPARAGED	VEERED	APPRECIATE	MERGE
BARREN	UKULELE	RAUCOUS	VACANT	RAPTURE

Stargirl Vocabulary

ISOSCELES	DORMANT	BIZARRE	CACTI	SHUN
MASSACRE	ANTIC	CONCEIVED	BLITHELY	EPISODE
TENTATIVELY	SWOON	FREE SPACE	ABSURDITY	ORATORICAL
HOAX	PRONE	SUBDUED	LINGER	VAMP
ALLEGIANCE	MARQUEE	TRANCE	FANATICS	CURIOUS

Stargirl Vocabulary

UKULELE	HESITATE	MESA	BAFFLE	DEVASTATION
APPRECIATE	GAPED	CONFOUND	SULLEN	MULL
MUNICIPAL	MERGE	FREE SPACE	ZEAL	PARANOID
BARREN	FACETIOUSLY	OBLIVIOUS	ELUSIVE	REVEL
NONCONFORMITY	PERPETUAL	ACQUIRED	DISPARAGED	SERENADED

Stargirl Vocabulary

MULL	APPLAUD	ACQUIRED	APPRECIATE	OBLIVIOUS
TENTATIVELY	MERGE	MANIA	RAUCOUS	ALLEGIANCE
ELUSIVE	MERINGUE	FREE SPACE	TRANCE	DISPARAGED
SERENADED	ZEAL	HESITATE	SWOON	MASSACRE
CURIOUS	CACTI	ANTIC	INTERROGATE	RAPTURE

Stargirl Vocabulary

REVEL	CONVERGING	BIZARRE	FACETIOUSLY	FANATICS
SUBDUED	UNCONVENTIONAL	MUNICIPAL	VAMP	SHUN
SULLEN	PERSISTED	FREE SPACE	UKULELE	CONCEIVED
LOTUS	GAPED	BLITHELY	LINGER	MARQUEE
EPISODE	PERPETUAL	NONCONFORMITY	BARREN	CONVINCED

Stargirl Vocabulary

LINGER	UNCONVENTIONAL	DEVASTATION	MANIA	PERPETUAL
PARANOID	FACETIOUSLY	ISOSCELES	ORATORICAL	MUNICIPAL
CACTI	ELUSIVE	FREE SPACE	SERENADED	SWOON
RAPTURE	VEERED	TENTATIVELY	PRONE	MASSACRE
CURIOUS	GAPED	RAUCOUS	CONFOUND	FANATICS

Stargirl Vocabulary

NONCONFORMITY	DISPARAGED	HESITATE	INTERROGATE	HOAX
ZEAL	UKULELE	MESA	EPISODE	SUBDUED
APPLAUD	ASPHALT	FREE SPACE	BLITHELY	TRANCE
BAFFLE	APPRECIATE	MARQUEE	VACANT	MERINGUE
SULLEN	ACQUIRED	ABSURDITY	OBLIVIOUS	SHUN

SUBDUED	MANIA	TENTATIVELY	LINGER	INTERROGATE
MESA	ANTIC	ISOSCELES	CACTI	RAPTURE
DISPARAGED	BAFFLE	FREE SPACE	PERSISTED	CURIOUS
MARQUEE	OBLIVIOUS	HESITATE	UNCONVENTIONAL	SULLEN
PRONE	GAPED	CONFOUND	ELUSIVE	ASPHALT

Stargirl Vocabulary

DEVASTATION	VAMP	MASSACRE	PARANOID	MULL
TRANCE	ACQUIRED	ALLEGIANCE	ABSURDITY	EPISODE
LOTUS	CONCEIVED	FREE SPACE	MERINGUE	PERPETUAL
UKULELE	NONCONFORMITY	SERENADED	MUNICIPAL	CONVINCED
ZEAL	SWOON	ORATORICAL	APPRECIATE	APPLAUD

Stargirl Vocabulary

OBLIVIOUS	CONVERGING	APPRECIATE	BLITHELY	RAPTURE
ASPHALT	EPISODE	ANTIC	ACQUIRED	CURIOUS
HOAX	SULLEN	FREE SPACE	PERPETUAL	VACANT
DISPARAGED	ABSURDITY	MULL	UKULELE	NONCONFORMITY
SWOON	INTERROGATE	HESITATE	MASSACRE	BAFFLE

Stargirl Vocabulary

ORATORICAL	MESA	VAMP	CONFOUND	UNCONVENTIONAL
DORMANT	FACETIOUSLY	FANATICS	GAPED	IMPULSE
PARANOID	LINGER	FREE SPACE	ZEAL	APPLAUD
CACTI	TRANCE	SERENADED	DEVASTATION	ALLEGIANCE
BARREN	MANIA	MERGE	RAUCOUS	CONVINCED

Stargirl Vocabulary

CONFOUND	BAFFLE	BLITHELY	DORMANT	CONVERGING
MERINGUE	MESA	INTERROGATE	DISPARAGED	LOTUS
IMPULSE	BIZARRE	FREE SPACE	CURIOUS	TRANCE
TENTATIVELY	RAUCOUS	CONVINCED	MULL	ACQUIRED
GAPED	ELUSIVE	LINGER	UNCONVENTIONAL	ASPHALT

Stargirl Vocabulary

MUNICIPAL	SWOON	UKULELE	HESITATE	VAMP
ORATORICAL	ALLEGIANCE	ISOSCELES	REVEL	SUBDUED
HOAX	PARANOID	FREE SPACE	DEVASTATION	NONCONFORMITY
ANTIC	MASSACRE	OBLIVIOUS	MANIA	SERENADED
ABSURDITY	VACANT	PERPETUAL	APPLAUD	CACTI

BARREN	FACETIOUSLY	PARANOID	DISPARAGED	UNCONVENTIONAL
CURIOUS	TENTATIVELY	ORATORICAL	NONCONFORMITY	LINGER
DORMANT	ZEAL	FREE SPACE	BIZARRE	TRANCE
HESITATE	MERGE	CONVERGING	CONFOUND	ALLEGIANCE
ISOSCELES	ASPHALT	ELUSIVE	OBLIVIOUS	VEERED

Stargirl Vocabulary

FANATICS	MULL	APPLAUD	MUNICIPAL	MERINGUE
LOTUS	APPRECIATE	SUBDUED	SHUN	SWOON
ACQUIRED	CONCEIVED	FREE SPACE	MANIA	INTERROGATE
VACANT	MASSACRE	PRONE	BAFFLE	ANTIC
SULLEN	DEVASTATION	RAPTURE	BLITHELY	IMPULSE

Stargirl Vocabulary

ISOSCELES	APPRECIATE	MARQUEE	PRONE	ZEAL
CONCEIVED	DISPARAGED	SERENADED	PERSISTED	REVEL
ABSURDITY	MULL	FREE SPACE	TENTATIVELY	DORMANT
UNCONVENTIONAL	ANTIC	CACTI	FANATICS	VEERED
CONVERGING	IMPULSE	RAPTURE	OBLIVIOUS	BAFFLE

Stargirl Vocabulary

ELUSIVE	SWOON	RAUCOUS	UKULELE	CURIOUS
SUBDUED	APPLAUD	ASPHALT	VACANT	LINGER
TRANCE	PARANOID	FREE SPACE	FACETIOUSLY	MESA
EPISODE	BLITHELY	PERPETUAL	MASSACRE	BARREN
GAPED	HESITATE	SULLEN	MERGE	ACQUIRED

SWOON	LINGER	BAFFLE	ACQUIRED	EPISODE
MERINGUE	MANIA	MASSACRE	PRONE	ORATORICAL
RAUCOUS	BIZARRE	FREE SPACE	MULL	PARANOID
ELUSIVE	ABSURDITY	APPLAUD	NONCONFORMITY	BLITHELY
CONVERGING	DORMANT	VACANT	GAPED	ASPHALT

Stargirl Vocabulary

HOAX	HESITATE	IMPULSE	APPRECIATE	SULLEN
ZEAL	INTERROGATE	SERENADED	ANTIC	CONVINCED
FACETIOUSLY	MARQUEE	FREE SPACE	ALLEGIANCE	CACTI
UKULELE	LOTUS	DISPARAGED	MUNICIPAL	REVEL
SHUN	CONCEIVED	FANATICS	MERGE	SUBDUED

ABSURDITY	TENTATIVELY	FANATICS	ELUSIVE	IMPULSE
TRANCE	UNCONVENTIONAL	LINGER	REVEL	ASPHALT
MARQUEE	MASSACRE	FREE SPACE	APPLAUD	ORATORICAL
HOAX	SERENADED	APPRECIATE	BIZARRE	DORMANT
PRONE	BLITHELY	PERPETUAL	ACQUIRED	MERGE

Stargirl Vocabulary

ZEAL	HESITATE	GAPED	MULL	CONCEIVED
SWOON	VACANT	BAFFLE	EPISODE	FACETIOUSLY
VAMP	MERINGUE	FREE SPACE	BARREN	SHUN
DEVASTATION	VEERED	RAPTURE	RAUCOUS	PERSISTED
CONVERGING	ISOSCELES	CONFOUND	ALLEGIANCE	ANTIC

Stargirl Vocabulary

UNCONVENTIONAL	ANTIC	SWOON	CONVERGING	MASSACRE
TENTATIVELY	HESITATE	DISPARAGED	PERPETUAL	CONVINCED
GAPED	DEVASTATION	FREE SPACE	MANIA	INTERROGATE
CONFOUND	HOAX	MESA	VEERED	SHUN
DORMANT	PARANOID	REVEL	MUNICIPAL	OBLIVIOUS

Stargirl Vocabulary

ALLEGIANCE	CURIOUS	BAFFLE	UKULELE	MERGE
ORATORICAL	VACANT	RAPTURE	TRANCE	ABSURDITY
VAMP	SERENADED	FREE SPACE	SUBDUED	ACQUIRED
EPISODE	MULL	PRONE	APPLAUD	NONCONFORMITY
FACETIOUSLY	SULLEN	APPRECIATE	MERINGUE	BARREN